Study Guide for

Essentials of
Managerial
Finance
Second Edition

and

Managerial
Finance
Third Edition

Study Guide for

Essentials of Managerial Finance

Second Edition

and

Managerial Finance

Third Edition

J. Fred Weston
University of California, Los Angeles

Eugene F. Brigham
The University of Wisconsin

Holt, Rinehart and Winston, Inc.
New York   Chicago   San Francisco   Atlanta
Dallas   Montreal   Toronto   London   Sydney

ISBN: 0-03-081469-3

Printed in the United States of America
3 4 5 6   090   9 8 7 6 5

Preface

Managerial Finance and *Essentials of Managerial Finance* are decision-oriented textbooks. Their central focus reflects the present-day emphasis on decisions affecting the value of the firm. This approach, which is more relevant than was the earlier descriptive approach, has the disadvantage from the student's point of view of being conceptually difficult. The *Study Guide* is designed to minimize this disadvantage.

Many instructors emphasize the problems found at the end of each chapter. There is a great deal of merit to this approach to finance, but it does have certain hazards. First, the time spent on problems is necessarily taken from time which could otherwise be spent on the text material. This increases the danger that the student will not fully comprehend the text materials, and to help combat this, the *Study Guide* provides an outline of each chapter. The outline should be examined prior to reading the chapter to obtain an overview of the material contained in the chapter, then also used later for review purposes. After having studied the chapter, the student can go over the outline, recalling relatively quickly the major points that were covered.

The second major feature of the *Study Guide* is the set of problems and solutions it provides. In the past, we have found certain difficulties in using the problem approach to teaching finance. Ideally, the students should be able to work the problems without an exorbitant expenditure of time, and the majority of the class should be able to reach a correct solution. This reduces the necessity of devoting much classroom time to the mechanics of the problem and permits more time to be spent discussing the basic points the problem illustrates. In practice, we find that students must spend an excessive amount of time solving the problem, and too often a large percentage of the class is unable to reach the correct solution. If the student spends too much time reaching the solution, then he has an insufficient amount of time left to think through the principles the problem is designed to illustrate. If a substantial number of students are unable to reach the correct solution, then the instructor must devote an inordinate amount of time to explaining the mechanics of the problem.

We have attempted to alleviate these difficulties by providing a sample set of problems and solutions in the *Study Guide.* The end-of-chapter problems give examples of most of the important points covered in the text. The problems and solutions provided in the *Study Guide* illustrate most of the end-of-chapter

v

problems. Therefore, if a student conscientiously works through the *Study Guide* problems, he should be able to complete most of the assigned end-of-chapter problems without difficulty.

The *Study Guide* follows the organization structure of *Essentials* exactly, but it differs somewhat from *Managerial Finance*. These differences are slight, and they will be readily apparent to the student and cause him no difficulty, but we should nevertheless point them out. First, this Second Edition of the *Study Guide* is a 1971 publication, whereas *Managerial Finance* was published in 1969. Such changes as the 1970 changes in the tax laws are reflected in the *Study Guide*, but not in *Managerial Finance*. In addition, we devised somewhat more effective ways of presenting some material since *Managerial Finance* was published—our method of explaining the cost of capital is an example—and these new procedures are used in the *Study Guide*. Finally, we made some slight changes in the structure of several chapters, but these changes will cause the student no difficulty.[1]

Although the purpose and general nature of this revised edition of the *Study Guide* are unchanged from the first edition, three years of experience in using the earlier version enable us to make certain important improvements. Since this book is designed strictly as an aid to students, we class-tested both the first *Study Guide* and the manuscript for this edition extensively, asking students for advice on how to make it most helpful to them. This trial-by-fire process helped us improve the organization and coverage of the material, and it also helped us eliminate arithmetic errors and inconsistencies that frequently creep into books such as this one.

In summary, this *Study Guide* is designed to enable the student to use his time more effectively and get more from the basic finance course. The chapter outline can be used to show what to look for in a chapter, and to facilitate study when reviewing for examinations. The problems and solutions can be used to help the student understand the mechanics of the various arithmetic operations involved in finance. He can refer to the solutions to check his own work, and can look over the solution when he is unable to solve an assigned problem relatively quickly. This enables him to determine the correct approach without an excessive amount of "spinning his wheels."

Los Angeles, California   J. Fred Weston
Madison, Wisconsin   Eugene F. Brigham
February 1971

---

[1]Specifically, Chapter 5 in *Managerial Finance* is treated in Chapters 5 and 6 in the *Study Guide*, and Chapters 13 and 14 in *Managerial Finance* are condensed into Chapter 14 of the *Study Guide*.

Contents

Study Guide for

*Essentials of
Managerial
Finance*
Second Edition

and

*Managerial
Finance*
Third Edition

Part I
Introduction

Chapter 1

Introduction: The Scope and Nature of Managerial Finance

Theme: A general overview of financial management as presented in this book is the concern of this chapter.

I. *The role of finance* within the firm has shifted through time:

A. Prior to 1920 finance focused on capital structure.

B. During the 1920s finance emphasized obtaining funds.

C. Following the severe recession of 1929-1933, with its wave of financial catastrophes, capital structure was again the preoccupation of finance.

D. In the early 1950s emphasis shifted to use of funds, with a focus on flows of funds and the internal management of the firm.

E. By the early 1960s the scope of finance was extended to policies and decisions which affect the value of the firm. The valuation of the business enterprise is determined largely by two factors:

1. Its expected stream of future earnings.

2. The riskiness of this earnings stream.

F. Beginning in 1966 the economy began to be greatly affected by inflation, tight money markets, and high costs of funds.

1. Obtaining funds became difficult.

2. Effective use of scarce and expensive funds further increased in significance the importance of finance.

3. The rise in debt ratios and the higher costs of debt made capital structures and debt repayment central considerations.

4. The cost of equity funds increased greatly, and increasing the value of the firm became critical for raising equity funds.

II. The shifting emphases in the study of finance can be attributed to major developments in the world economies and in the internal operations of business firms.

A. Some of these developments are listed:

1. Rise of large-scale business units.

2. Extensive product and market diversification.

3. Growth of research and development spending.

4. Increased emphasis on growth of the economy.
5. Rapid progress in transportation and communication.
6. Narrowing profit margins and intense competition.
7. Revolution in information processing.
8. Management science techniques.
9. Protracted international tensions.

B. Some impacts of these developments on the firm include:
1. Large-scale, decentralized operations have become commonplace.
2. The development of new techniques of financial management is taking place.
3. Firms need to finance a high rate of growth.
4. International operations have expanded.
5. Planning and control are becoming increasingly important.
   a. Overall and departmental profit goals are established.
   b. Results are measured against standards.
6. There is greater use of computer-assisted managerial decision-making.
7. More use is made of formal quantitative models in financial analysis and decisions, including linear programming, game theory, and simulation.
8. Firms are faced with a worldwide financial capital shortage and high costs of funds.

III. Organization of *Essentials of Managerial Finance.*
A. This book deals with three closely connected areas:
1. The theory of finance.
2. The development of financial decision models.
3. Descriptive and institutional material.

B. These three interrelated areas are reflected in the following broad types of subject matter (the major parts of the book):
1. The Tax Environment.
2. Financial Analyses, Planning, and Control.
3. Long-term Investment Decisions.
4. Valuation and Financial Structure.
5. Working Capital Management.
6. Long-term Financing.
7. Valuation in Mergers and Corporate Readjustments.
8. An Integrated View of Financial Management.

C. Because of the requirements for effective financial management in a changing economic environment, equal emphasis is given to the four major aspects of the finance functions that have been its individual focus in previous time periods:
1. Financial planning and control.
   a. Planning involves the formulation of objectives and the selection of alternative courses of action.

b. Control involves assuming responsibility for the completion of plans and for increased efficiency in their execution.
2. Fixed investment decisions.
3. Management of working capital.
4. Individual financing episodes to achieve financial structures which reflect a balance between *profitability* and *risk.*
D. All of the above is encompassed in the goal of maximizing the value of the ownership securities of the firm.
IV. The orientation of *Essentials of Managerial Finance* is presented below:
A. *Insider versus outsider view.* The internal view receives primary emphasis because of the managerial orientation of this book.
B. *Small firm versus large firm.* Principles of managerial finance are generally applicable to both small and large firms. Some of the factual and institutional materials may differ, and the nature of the problems may differ in degree, but not in their fundamentals.
C. *Profit-making versus non-profit-making organizations.*
1. Since we live in a world of scarce resources, a pervasive problem is the efficient use of resources.
2. The problem of obtaining funds and their efficient utilization faces all purposive organizations.
3. The managerial techniques of financial analysis, planning, control, and effective management of fund flows are generally applicable. Many of the aspects of valuation are reflected in cost-benefit analysis, employed by both profit and non-profit organizations; and the recent developments of program budgeting in governmental organizations represent the application of the principles of financing planning and control found in managerial finance.
V. The place of finance in the organization.
A. Usually the financial manager is a member of the first level of the corporate staff in a large organization.
B. The financial manager occupies a top-level position for these reasons:
1. The planning, analysis, and control operations for which he is responsible are of critical importance to the firm.
2. Many financial decisions affect the survival of the firm.
3. Significant economies may be realized through centralization of financial operations.
C. In addition to strategic, long-term decisions, a large number of day-to-day operations are performed by financial officers:
1. Handling cash receipts and disbursements.
2. Borrowing from commercial banks on a regular and continuing basis.
3. Formulating cash budgets.
VI. Finance performs a crucial role in the success and survival of the firm.

A. Financial decisions both past and present affect the viability and control of the firm.
B. Financing is the critical management function in that it provides the means of remedying weak management in other areas.
C. However, since money alone can never substitute for other operating strengths, finance is an interdependent part in the totality of managerial functions and responsibilities affecting an organization's performance.

PROBLEMS

There are no problems for Chapter 1.

Chapter 2

The Tax Environment

Theme: Government plays an increasingly important role in business and economic life. One of the significant areas of impact is taxation. Since most business decisions are influenced by tax factors, this chapter provides a summary of the basic elements of our tax structure and shows how they relate to financial decisions.

I. *Fiscal policy* involves altering the level and composition of government receipts and expenditures to influence the level of economic activity. Two principal methods of changing tax receipts are employed presently:

A. *Changing tax rates.*

1. An *increase* in tax rates reduces personal disposable incomes and corporate after-tax profits. This, in turn, (a) reduces each individual's purchasing power and demand for goods; (b) lowers the profitability of new investments; and (c) reduces funds available for investment.

2. A *decrease* in tax rates has the opposite effect, stimulating economic expansion.

3. Tax rates change infrequently because Congress is reluctant to take such action.

B. *Accelerated depreciation.*

1. Depreciation charges are deductible for federal income tax purposes.

2. If a more rapid or accelerated depreciation is allowed for tax purposes, tax payments are lower and business is encouraged.

   a. Accelerated depreciation increases corporate cash flows and makes more funds available for investment.

   b. Faster cash flows increase the rate of return on investments.

3. Depreciation methods are determined by the Congress, which recently passed major changes in depreciation laws.

   a. In 1954 two accelerated depreciation methods were permitted:

      1. Sum-of-years-digits method.

      2. Double declining balance method.

   b. In 1962 the depreciable lives of assets, for tax purposes, were reduced.

II. The corporate income tax structure has wide implications for business planning.

  A. Since corporations pay 22 percent on their first $25,000 of taxable income, and 48 percent on such income over $25,000, there are limited tax benefits from separating companies into two or more separate corporations in order to hold the income of each unit under $25,000.

    1. This indeed has been a practice of some firms in the past.

    2. The Tax Reform Act of 1969 was aimed at abolishing the tax savings from this practice.

      a. It limited the advantages of multiple corporations from 1970 to 1974.

      b. It abolished all such advantages beginning in 1975.

  B. Corporate capital gains and losses affect the decision as to whether a firm should incorporate.

    1. Capital gains and losses are profits and losses on the sale of capital assets—those assets, such as security investments, which are not bought and sold in the ordinary course of business.

    2. Real and depreciable property used in the business is not defined as a capital asset. However, profits made on the disposal of such property may be treated as capital gains, and losses are deductible from ordinary income.

    3. An asset must be held at least six months to produce a long-term gain. While net short-term gains are taxed at regular corporate income tax rates, net long-term capital gains are subject to a maximum tax of 30 percent.

  C. Depreciable assets' treatment affects investment decisions.

    1. The cost of an asset subject to depreciation is defined as the original purchase price less accumulated depreciation, that is, its book value.

    2. Sale of such an asset *for more than its book value* may result in either a capital gain or an ordinary gain for tax purposes.
That part of the gain which equals depreciation taken is taxed as ordinary income (recapture of depreciation).
Any amount of profit over the accumulated depreciation is taxed as a capital gain.

    3. If the sale of such an asset results in a net loss (the cost less depreciation incurred less the sale price), the net loss can be deducted from ordinary income.

  D. Although a net capital loss on nondepreciable assets is not deductible from ordinary income, it may be carried back three years, then forward for five years, and used to offset capital gains for that period.

  E. To avoid multiple taxation of corporate income 85 percent of dividends received by one corporation from another is exempt from taxation.

  F. While *interest payments* by a corporation *are* a deductible expense to the firm, *dividends* paid by a corporation *are not* deductible by the firm.

  G. Firms must estimate their taxable income and pay taxes quarterly.

H. Net operating income carry-back and carry-forward aids corporations whose income fluctuates widely by permitting income averaging of a sort.
  1. Losses may be carried back three years, then forward for five years.
  2. Adjustments begin with carry-back to the earliest year.
 I. If a corporation retains earnings to avoid dividends which would be subject to personal income taxes, these retained earnings are subject to penalty rates under the *improperly accumulated income* section of the Internal Revenue Code.
III. Personal income taxes have an important effect on business decisions.
  A. More than 80 percent of all firms in the U.S. are organized as individual proprietorships or as partnerships, not as corporations; the income of these firms is taxed as personal income to the owners or partners.
  B. The personal income tax rate structure is lower than the corporate tax rate at lower incomes, but at higher incomes the corporate rate is lower. This influences business decisions as to whether to be taxed as corporations or as proprietorships or partnerships.
    1. The personal income tax rate structure is progressive.
    2. Joint returns by married couples are permitted.
    3. Through 1970, on joint returns, the tax rate for individuals started at 14 percent and rose to 70 percent on all taxable income over $200,000.
    4. On *earned income* (salaries and so on, as opposed to income from property), the maximum rate on both single and joint returns is limited to 60 percent in 1971 and to 50 percent thereafter.
    5. The maximum rate remains at 70 percent on other personal income—for example, income from rentals, stocks, or bonds.
    6. A surtax of 10 percent was in effect from April 1, 1968, through December 31, 1969; a 5 percent surtax was imposed from January 1, 1970, to June 30, 1970.
  C. Personal capital gains and losses, like those of corporations, are separated as to short term and long term by the six-month holding period.
    1. Net short-term gains are taxed at regular rates.
    2. Net long-term gains of up to $50,000 are taxed at the lower of 25 percent or the ordinary rate on one-half the net long-term gains. One-half of all capital gains over $50,000 are taxed as ordinary income.
    3. Fifty percent of net capital losses up to a limit of $2,000 may be deducted against ordinary income. Thus, the maximum deduction in a given year is $1,000. Capital losses may be carried forward until exhausted.

PROBLEMS

2-1. A corporation has taxable income of $75,000.
  a. What is the tax bill?
  b. What is the marginal tax rate?

Solution:

a.
	22%	×	$25,000	= $ 5,500
	48%	×	50,000	= 24,000
Taxable income			$75,000	$29,500, tax bill

b. The marginal tax rate is 48 percent.

2-2. A firm has income (before interest, dividends, and taxes) of $200,000. Interest expense is $10,000 and preferred dividend payments are $30,000. What is the tax bill?

Solution:

Operating income	$200,000
Less: Interest expense	−10,000
Taxable income	$190,000

Tax payable
$ 25,000 × 22% = $ 5,500
$165,000 × 48% = $79,200
Tax bill $84,700

2-3. A firm has ordinary income of $150,000 and receives in addition corporate dividend income of $45,000. What is the tax bill?

Solution:

Dividend income	$ 45,000
Less: dividend exclusion:	
.85 × $45,000	−38,250
Taxable dividends	$ 6,750
plus: ordinary income	150,000
Total taxable income	$156,750

Tax payable
$ 25,000 × 22% = $ 5,500
$131,750 × 48% = $63,240
Tax bill $68,740

2-4. An individual has ordinary income of $80,000 after deductions and long-term capital gains of $15,000. If his average tax rate is 35 percent on the $80,000 and his marginal tax rate is 45 percent, his lowest possible tax will be _____.

Solution:

Option 1 (ordinary tax rate on one-half capital gain)
$$
\begin{array}{lcl}
\$80,000 \ (0.35) & = & \$28,000 \\
\text{½} \ (\$15,000) \ (0.45) & = & \underline{+3,375} \\
& & \$31,375
\end{array}
$$

Option 2 (25 percent rate on entire capital gain)
$$
\begin{array}{lcl}
\$80,000 \ (0.35) & = & \$28,000 \\
15,000 \ (0.30) & = & \underline{+4,500} \\
& & \$32,500
\end{array}
$$

Note: Option 1 is always preferable to option 2 if the individual is in a marginal tax bracket less than 50 percent.

2-5. A corporation had a $7,880 tax bill this year. What were its taxable earnings?

Solution:

Step 1:	Total tax bill			$ 7,880
	Less: 22% of $25,000			5,500
	Equals: 48% of earnings (in excess of $25,000)			$ 2,380
Step 2:	Taxable income at 48%	=	($2,380/0.48) =	$ 4,958
	Taxable income at 22%	=	($5,500/0.22) =	25,000
	Total taxable income			$29,958

2-6. A mirror manufacturer had ordinary income of $150,000 this year. During the year, the firm sold off capital assets (acquired three months earlier) for a net capital gain of $100,000. Other capital assets (acquired two years earlier) were sold off to net a gain of $200,000. What is the firm's tax bill?

Solution:

Ordinary income $150,000:	$ 25,000	X	22%	=	$ 5,500
	+125,000	X	48%	=	+ 60,000
	$150,000				$ 65,500
Short-term capital gain:	$100,000	X	48%	=	$ 48,000
Long-term capital gain:	$200,000	X	30%	=	$ 60,000
			Tax bill	=	$173,500

2-7. Al Smith is a married man with two children. His gross income for 1971 is $11,500, which includes $4,450 of corporate dividends received by his wife. He takes the standard deduction. What is his taxable income for the year, and what is his tax bill?

Solution:

a. $11,500, gross income
   $\underline{-100}$, dividend exclusion on wife's stock
   $11,400

b. $11,400
   $\underline{-1,500}$, standard deduction
   $ 9,900

c. $ 9,900
   $\underline{-2,600}$, four exemptions at $650 each
   $\underline{\underline{$ 7,300}}$, taxable income

d. Tax:*   Tax on $4,000 $ 620.00
               Tax on add'l income:
               (19% of $3,300) $\underline{$ 627.00}$
                                         $\underline{\underline{$1,247.00}}$

   *Use Table 2-3, joint returns.

 2-8. The taxable income of Collins Corporation, formed in 1970, is as follows (losses in parentheses).

1970	$(450,000)
1971	200,000
1972	325,000
1973	350,000
1974	(200,000)

What is Collins' tax payment each year after carry-forwards and carry-backs are accounted for?

Solution:

Year	Income	Less forward	Carry-back	Income before tax	Tax on up to $25,000	Excess of $25,000	Total tax	Tax refund resulting from carry-back
1970	$(450,000)							
1971	200,000	450,000						
1972	325,000	250,000		75,000	5,500	24,000	29,500	
1973	350,000			350,000	5,500	156,000	161,500	
1974	(200,000)		(200,000)					89,500*

*Calculation of 1974 tax refund:
  $75,000 carried back to 1972 for refund of entire $29,500 taxes paid
$125,000 carry back to 1973 for refund of $60,000 ($125,000 X 0.48)
     $29,500
     $\underline{+60,000}$
     $\underline{$89,500}$ total tax refund.

2-9. This year Company A expects taxable income of $300,000. Company B forecasts a $60,000 loss for the year. If the two firms merge before the end of the year, how much will be generated in tax savings?

Solution:

a. Separately:	*Company A*	*Company B*
Taxable income	$300,000	$(60,000)
Tax payable		
$25,000 @ 22% =	5,500	
275,000 @ 48% =	132,000	
Tax bill	$137,500	–0–

b. Merged:

Taxable income of A company	$300,000
Taxable Income of B company	(60,000)
New taxable Income	$240,000

Tax payable

$ 25,000 @ 22% =	$ 5,500
$215,000 @ 48% =	$103,200
Tax bill	$108,700

c.

Separate Tax bill	$137,500
Less: Merged tax bill	–108,700
Tax Saving due to merger	$ 28,800

Part II
Financial Analysis, Planning, and Control

See Notes

Theme: Ratio analysis is basic to understanding and evaluating the results of business operations. It provides a framework on which the financial manager can plan his future financial requirements.

I. Financial ratios may be classified into four fundamental types:

A. *Liquidity ratios* measure the firm's ability to meet its maturing short-term obligations.

The current ratio (current assets divided by current liabilities) is a generally accepted measure of short-term solvency.

1. Current assets include cash, marketable securities, accounts receivable, and inventories.
2. Current liabilities consist of accounts payable, short-term notes payable, current maturities of long-term debt, accrued income taxes, and other accrued expenses.

The quick ratio, or acid test, is calculated by deducting inventories from current assets and dividing the remainder by current liabilities. This ratio measures short-term solvency, but removes inventories from the calculation because inventories are the least liquid of a firm's current assets and their liquidation frequently results in losses.

B. *Leverage ratios* measure the extent to which the firm has been financed by debt. Creditors look to the equity to provide a margin of safety, but by raising funds through debt, owners gain the benefits of maintaining control of the firm with a limited investment. If a firm earns more on borrowed funds than it pays in interest, the return to the owners is magnified.

The debt-to-total-assets ratio measures the percentage of total funds that have been provided by creditors.

1. The lower the ratio, the greater the protection against creditors' losses in the event of liquidation.
2. Owners may seek high leverage either to magnify earnings or because raising new equity means giving up some degree of control.

The times-interest-earned ratio (net income before interest and taxes divided by interest charges) measures the extent to which earnings can decline without resultant financial embarassment to the firm because of inability to meet annual interest costs.

Fixed charge coverage (net income available for fixed charges) generalizes the preceding ratio by adding fixed charges such as rent payments to interest payments for calculating the fixed obligations of the company.

C. Activity ratios measure how effectively a firm is using its resources.

Inventory turnover (sales or costs of goods sold divided by average inventory) measures the efficiency of inventory utilization.

1. A high inventory turnover demonstrates that a company does not hold excessive stocks of inventory.
2. The average inventory figure should be adjusted if the firm's business is highly seasonal or if there has been a strong upward or downward sales trend during the year.

The average collection period (receivables divided by sales per day) is compared to the terms on which the firm sells its goods. This measures efficiency in collection of accounts receivable.

1. Sales per day equals annual credit sales divided by 360 days.
2. The average collection period should be supplemented with the aging schedule. This groups accounts receivable according to how long they have been outstanding.

The sales-to-fixed-assets ratio (sales divided by fixed assets) measures the turnover of capital assets or the efficiency of fixed assets; a low ratio indicates idle capacity of assets.

Total assets turnover (sales divided by total assets) measures the overall utilization of assets. A low ratio indicates that the company is not generating a sufficient volume of business for the size of its asset investment.

D. Profitability ratios measure management's overall effectiveness as shown by the returns generated on sales and investment. *The profit margin* on sales (net profit after taxes divided by sales) gives the profit per dollar of sales.

1. This ratio indicates the degree to which sales prices can decline before causing an overall loss.
2. A profit margin somewhat below the industry average indicates that the firm's sales prices are relatively low or that its costs are relatively high, or both.

Net profit to total assets measures the return on the firm's total investment.

1. Sometimes interest costs are added to net profits after taxes to form the numerator of the ratio.
2. A low ratio can result from a low profit margin on sales, or from a low turnover of total assets, or both.

The net-profit-after-taxes-to-net-worth ratio indicates the rate of return on the stockholders' investment.

II. *Trend analysis* involves computing the ratios of a particular firm for several years and comparing the ratios over time to see whether the firm is improving or deteriorating. *Comparative analysis* is comparing the key ratios of the firm with those of other similar firms in the industry, or with an industry average.

III. *The du Pont system of financial analysis* reveals the manner in which activity ratios and profit margins on sales interact to determine the profitability of assets.

A. The modified du Pont control chart pictured in Figure 3-1 encompasses many factors. The chart illustrates, among other things, that profits and return on investment depend upon control of costs and investment. If costs are too high, profit margins on sales fall. If investment is not controlled, the turnover (sales to net operating assets) declines.

B. Profit planning depends to a great extent upon control of costs and turnover of investment.

1. Cost control requires detailed study of the operations of the individual business firm.

2. The importance of turnover for determining return on total investment is shown by the following relationship:

$$\frac{\text{sales}}{\text{investment}} \times \frac{\text{profit}}{\text{sales}} = \frac{\text{profit}}{\text{investment}}$$

3. The turnover concept can be extended to show how leverage affects the return on net worth. This is shown by the relationships in Table 3-1.

TABLE 3-1   Turnover, profit margins, and returns on net worth, 1966

	Sales to total assets		Profit to sales	Net worth to total assets	Profit to net worth*
All manufacturing firms	1.60	X	5.6%	59%	15.2%
Hercules, Inc. (chemical producer)	1.15		8.5	68	14.4
Safeway Stores (food retailer)	5.23		1.8	60	15.6

*The figures in this column may be found as:

$$\text{profit to net worth} = \frac{\text{sales}}{\text{total assets}} \times \frac{\text{profit}}{\text{sales}} \div \frac{\text{net worth}}{\text{total assets}}$$

SOURCES: Moody's Investors Service; SEC-FTC *Bulletins*; Robert Morris Associates; *Annual Statement Studies*.

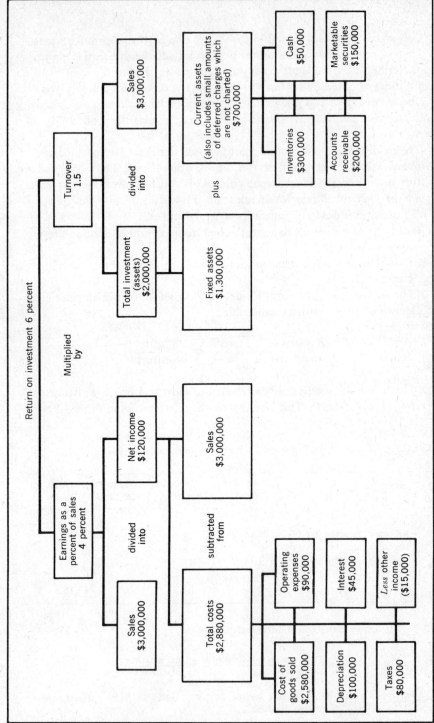

FIGURE 3-1. Modified du Pont system of financial control

C. There are critical checkpoints in the du Pont system.
1. The system is applied to divisions, products, or other profit centers.
2. Profit center performance is used to allocate additional resources. Naturally, resources are funneled into the profit centers that are contributing the highest return on investment.
3. The use of the du Pont system for control purposes is discussed in more detail in Chapter 6.
D. The du Pont system can be extended to include leverage.
1. The following formula shows how financial leverage can be used to increase the rate of return on net worth.

$$\text{percentage return on net worth} = \frac{\text{(turnover) times (profit margin on sales)}}{\text{percent of assets financed by net worth}}$$

2. Limitations to the use of leverage are twofold:
a. Creditors refuse to supply funds when high leverage ratios are attained.
b. High leverage ratios increase the risk of bankruptcy to the firm.
IV. Financial ratios are useful in credit analysis.
A. It may be necessary to calculate many ratios or only a few to provide a picture of the state of the firm.
B. Among the qualitative factors considered by the credit manager are the economic position of the customer firm and its managerial qualities, as well as his own firm's profit margin.
C. Abbreviated analysis is used in credit decisions involving a large number of customers per day:
1. The current ratio is calculated to determine the degree of pressing burdens of short-term debt.
2. The total debt-to-assets ratio is calculated to determine the extent of debt financing.
3. Inadequate equity often results in a current ratio that is too low.
4. Excessive debt usually results in slow payments.
5. The decision to grant credit to a marginal credit risk rests heavily on whether the profitability ratio is high enough to bring the customer to a current payment position in the foreseeable future.
V. Financial ratios are useful in security analysis.
A. The principal emphasis is on the long-run profit potential of the firm.
B. The focus is, therefore, on activity and profitability ratios.
VI. Financial ratios are used by the financial manager.
A. The number and kinds of ratios actually used by the financial manager will depend upon the nature of the industry and the size and age of the firm.
B. Financial ratios are not to be used as mechanical rules on which to base decisions; rather, they should be viewed as helpful pieces of information to be used in conjunction with the manager's assessment of men and future events.

PROBLEMS

3-1. The financial statements of Snowfield Appliance Company for 1969, 1970, and 1971 follow. The norms of the financial ratios given below for the household appliance industry are from Dun & Bradstreet.

   a. Fill in the blanks.

   b. What management problems are reflected in these financial data during each of the following years: 1969? 1970? 1971?

The Snowfield Appliance Company—Comparative balance sheets for years 1969-1971

Assets	1969	1970	1971
Cash	$ 5,000	$ 4,000	$10,000
Receivables, net	25,000	15,000	15,000
Inventories	22,000	34,000	25,000
Total current assets	$52,000	$53,000	$50,000
Net property	25,000	25,000	26,000
Other assets	2,000	2,000	2,000
Total assets	$79,000	$80,000	$78,000

Liabilities and capital			
Accounts payable	$10,000	$12,000	$12,000
Notes payable (5%)	7,000	7,000	7,000
Other current liabilities	3,000	1,000	2,000
Total current liabilities	$20,000	$20,000	$21,000
Long-term debt (6%)	15,000	15,000	15,000
Net worth	44,000	45,000	42,000
Total claims on assets	$79,000	$80,000	$78,000

	1969		1970		1971	
Sales		$120,000		$110,000		$130,000
Material	$45,000		$39,000		$47,000	
Labor	40,500		37,000		43,000	
Heat, light, and power	9,000		9,000		9,000	
Depreciation (10%)	1,500	96,000	1,500	86,500	1,500	100,500
Gross profit		24,000		23,500		29,500
Selling expenses	10,000		10,000		10,000	
General and administrative expenses	9,500	19,500	9,250	19,250	8,750	18,750
Operating profit		4,500		4,250		10,750
Less: Interest expenses		1,250		1,250		1,250
Net profit before taxes		3,250		3,000		9,500
Federal income taxes		1,625		1,500		4,750
Net income		$ 1,625		$ 1,500		$ 4,750

		1969		1970		1971	
		Company Ratio	*Average Ratio*	*Company Ratio*	*Average Ratio*	*Company Ratio*	*Average Ratio*
1.	$\dfrac{\text{Current assets}}{\text{Current liabilities}}$	_____	2.5 times	_____	2.6 times	_____	2.7 times
2.	$\dfrac{\text{Sales}}{\text{Inventory (at book)}}$	_____	4.6 times	_____	4.8 times	_____	5.0 times
3.	Collection period (days)	_____	53.0 days	_____	51.0 days	_____	48.0 days
4.	$\dfrac{\text{Net profit}}{\text{Sales}}$	_____	3.4%	_____	3.5%	_____	3.7%
5.	$\dfrac{\text{Net profit}}{\text{Net worth}}$	_____	10.0%	_____	10.2%	_____	10.5%
6.	$\dfrac{\text{Net profit}}{\text{Total assets}}$	_____	4.3%	_____	4.9%	_____	5.7%

Solution:

The Snowfield Appliance Company—Financial ratios

	1969	*Norm*	*1970*	*Norm*	*1971*	*Norm*
1. Current ratios	2.6	2.5 times	2.7	2.6 times	2.4	2.7 times
2. Inventory turnover	5.5	4.6 times	3.2	4.8 times	5.2	5.0 times
3. Collection period	75.0	53.0 days	49.0	51.0 days	42.0	48.0 days
4. Net profit to sales	1.4	3.4%	1.4	3.5%	3.7	3.7%
5. Net profit to net worth	3.7	10.0%	3.3	10.2%	11.3	10.5%
6. Net profit to total assets	2.1	4.3%	1.9	4.9%	6.1	5.7%

During 1969, the Snowfield Appliance Company had a poor collection policy. This was evident in that the average collection period was about one and one-half times the norm for the industry. Because of the poor collection policy, the profit ratios were also low. By 1970, although the collection policy had been remedied, the inventory policies were poor. This is evident in the inventory ratio. The turnover is much less than the norm for the industry. The statement for 1971 shows that the company has overcome most of the major difficulties and compares reasonably well with the norms for the household appliance industry.

3-2. Determine the sales of a firm with the financial data given below.

Current ratio	2.5
Quick ratio	2.0
Current liabilities	$600,000
Inventory turnover	4 times

Solution:

a. $\dfrac{\text{current assets}}{\$600,000} = 2.5$

current assets = $1,500,000

b. $\dfrac{\text{current assets} - \text{inventory}}{\$600,000} = 2.0$

current assets − inventory = $1,200,000

inventory = $ 300,000

c. $\dfrac{\text{sales}}{\text{inventory}}$ = inventory turnover

$\dfrac{\text{sales}}{\$300,000} = 4$

sales = $1,200,000

3-3. Complete the balance sheet and sales data (fill in the blanks), using the following financial data:

Debt/net worth	60 percent
Acid test ratio	1.2/1.0
Asset turnover	1.5 times
Days sales outstanding in accounts receivable	40 days
Gross profit margin	30 percent
Inventory turnover (at cost)	6 times

Balance sheet

Cash	_____	Accounts payable	_____
Accounts receivable	_____	Common stock	$15,000
Inventories	_____	Retained earnings	$22,000
Plant and equipment	_____		
		Total liabilities	
Total assets	_____	and capital	_____
Sales	_____		
Cost of goods sold	_____		

Solution:

a. $\dfrac{\text{debt}}{\text{net worth}} = \dfrac{\text{debt}}{37,000} = 60\%; \text{debt} = \$22,200$

b. $37,000

   $\underline{\quad 22,200}$

   $\underline{\underline{\$59,200}}$, total assets

c. acid test = $1.2 = \dfrac{\text{cash} + \text{A/R}}{\text{current liabilities}} = \dfrac{\text{cash} + \text{A/R}}{22,200}$

   cash + A/R = $26,640

d. asset turnover = $1.5 = \dfrac{\text{sales}}{\text{assets}} = \dfrac{\text{sales}}{59,200}$

   sales = 88,800

e. days sales outstanding in accounts receivable = $40; 40/360 \times 88,800$

   = 9,867 accounts receivable

f. cash = cash + A/R − A/R = $26,640

   $\underline{\quad -\ 9,867}$

   $\$16,773$, cash

g. gross profit margin = 30 percent

   cost of goods sold = 70 percent × sales

   $88,800

   $\underline{\times\ 0.70}$

   $62,160, cost of goods sold

h. inventory turnover (at cost) = 6

   $\dfrac{\text{sales}}{\text{inventories}} = \dfrac{\$88,800}{\text{inventories}} = 6$

   inventories = $14,800

i. cash $16,773

   A/R   9,867

   inventories $\underline{\quad 14,800}$

   $41,440

   total assets   59,200

   $\underline{-41,440}$

   $17,760, plant and equipment

Theme: In addition to the ratios described in the preceding chapter, the financial manager has other tools available to aid in profit planning and control: break-even analysis, analysis of operating leverage, and sources and uses of funds statements.

I. Break-even analysis is an important tool for profit planning.
  A. It provides information on the volume of sales at which total revenues begin to cover total costs fully.
  B. The practical significance is that break-even analysis guides the manager in the comparison of prices, expected volume, and the required volume to cover total costs.
  C. Figure 4-1 illustrates break-even analysis, as do the tables and related materials that follow it:
    1. Relations among units produced, total variable costs, fixed costs, total costs, and total income:

Units sold	Total variable costs	Fixed costs	Total costs	Total sales	Net profit (loss)
20,000	$ 24,000	$40,000	$ 64,000	$ 40,000	$(24,000)
40,000	48,000	40,000	88,000	80,000	(8,000)
50,000	60,000	40,000	100,000	100,000	—
60,000	72,000	40,000	112,000	120,000	8,000
80,000	96,000	40,000	136,000	160,000	24,000
100,000	120,000	40,000	160,000	200,000	40,000
120,000	144,000	40,000	184,000	240,000	56,000
140,000	168,000	40,000	208,000	280,000	72,000

    2. Formula using totals:
      a. $\dfrac{\text{total fixed costs}}{1 - \dfrac{\text{total variable costs}}{\text{total sales volume}}} = \text{break-even point}$

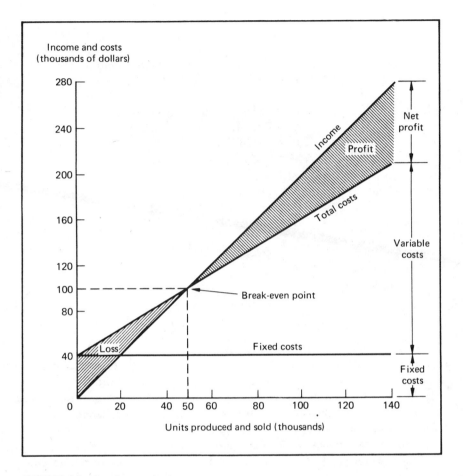

FIGURE 4-1   Break-even chart

b. Illustration in table above:
   1. For lowest sales volume shown in table:

$$\frac{\$40,000}{1 - \dfrac{24,000}{40,000}} = \frac{\$40,000}{1 - .6} = \$100,000$$

   2. For highest volume shown in table:

$$\frac{\$40,000}{1 - \dfrac{168,000}{280,000}} = \frac{\$40,000}{1 - .6} = \$100,000$$

3. Algebraic solution to break-even volume:

    a. The break-even quantity is defined as that volume of output at which revenue is just equal to total costs (fixed costs plus variable costs).

    b. Let:

$$P = \text{sales price per unit}$$
$$Q = \text{quantity produced and sold}$$
$$F = \text{fixed costs}$$
$$V = \text{variable costs per unit}$$

    c. Then:

$$P \times Q = F + V \times Q$$
$$P \times Q - V \times Q = F$$
$$Q(P - V) = F$$
$$Q = \frac{F}{P - V} \text{ at break-even } Q$$

    d. Illustration:

$$Q = \frac{\$40{,}000}{\$2.00 - \$1.20}$$
$$= 50{,}000 \text{ units}$$

II. Among specific uses of break-even analysis are the following:

  A. In new product decisions, break-even analysis will indicate how large a sales volume the new product must attain in order to realize a profit.

  B. To study the effects of a general expansion in the level of operations, break-even points are calculated on the basis of total sales (in dollar amounts rather than in units of output) and total costs.

  C. In assessing a modernization or automation program, break-even analysis indicates the degree to which a firm may profitably utilize operating leverage.

III. *Operating leverage* is defined as the extent to which fixed costs are used in operations. High fixed costs arise from employing larger amounts of capital, thus permitting the firm to operate with reduced labor and smaller variable costs.

  A. The degree of operating leverage (*OL*) at a specified volume of operations, or the elasticity of operating leverage, is:

$$OL = \frac{\text{Percentage change in Net Operating Income } (NOI)}{\text{Percentage change in Output (Quantity Sold)}}$$

  B. This can also be expressed in a form analogous to point elasticity:

$$\text{Degree of operating leverage} = OL = \frac{S - VC}{S - VC - FC}$$

Where S = Sales
                  VC = Variable Costs
                  FC = Fixed Costs

C. Figure 4-2 illustrates the effects of variations in operating leverage.
D. Calculations for the degree of operating leverage involve the following steps:
  1. Operating leverage is measured by the ratio of the percentage change in net operating income (*NOI*) to the percentage changes in output (quantity sold). *OL* is calculated for the three firms shown in Figure 4-2, as units sold increase from 80,000 to 100,000 units, an increase of 25 percent:

	Firm A	Firm B	Firm C
NOI at 80,000 units	24,000	20,000	20,000
NOI at 100,000 units	40,000	30,000	40,000
Percent change in NOI	67%	50%	100%
Percent change in output	25%	25%	25%
Operating leverage (OL)	2.7	2.0	4.0

  2. Operating leverage at 80,000 units of output is measured by the point elasticity formula:

$$OL = \frac{S - VC}{S - VC - FC}$$

Firm A   *Firm B*

$$\frac{\$160,000 - 96,000}{\$160,000 - 96,000 - 40,000} \qquad \frac{160,000 - 120,000}{160,000 - 120,000 - 20,000}$$

$$OL = 2.7 \qquad\qquad\qquad OL = 2$$

Firm C

$$\frac{160,000 - 80,000}{160,000 - 80,000 - 60,000}$$

$$OL = 4$$

  3. This is significant for the following reasons:
    a. The relative influence of fixed costs in operations is affected by (1) price changes, (2) changes in variable costs, and (3) changes in the relative importance of fixed costs.
    b. The higher the degree of operating leverage, the greater the impact of a given percentage change in output on net operating income *in both directions*.

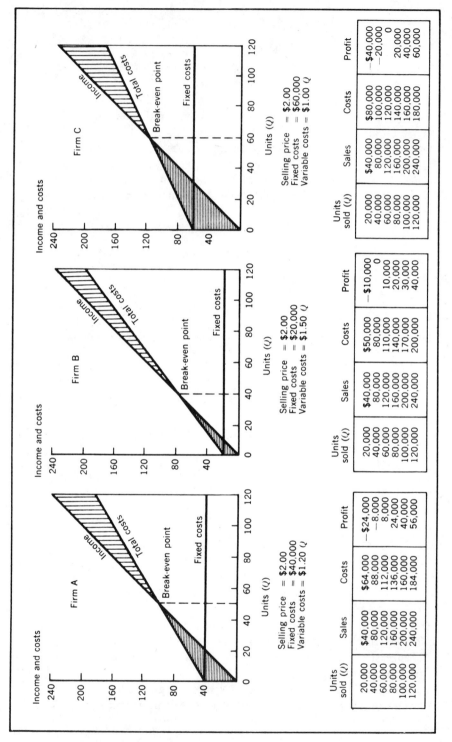

FIGURE 4-2 Operating leverage

c. The degree of operating leverage (*OL*) influences decisions on the amount of financial leverage the firm employs because financial and operating leverage jointly affect the variability of the firm's earnings. This interaction is discussed in Chapter 10.

IV. There are limitations to linear break-even analysis.

A. Some have to do with demand.

1. Linear relationships assume that the quantity demanded is independent of price.

2. However, price change effects can be exhibited by having a different total income line for each price.

3. Alternatively, a curved total income line implies that prices may have to be changed to achieve a higher volume. (See Figure 4-3)

B. Other limitations relate to costs.

1. Some costs are semifixed and, hence, also semivariable.

2. As the scale of plant is changed, a step type of cost function results.

3. At larger scales of operation, further economies and higher returns from both the fixed and variable factors may be achieved, but later on capacity is strained, so that the total cost curve first increases at a decreasing rate, then increases at an increasing rate. Figure 4-3 illustrates such a cost curve.

V. Nonlinear break-even analysis as illustrated in Figure 4-3 is intellectually appealing. However, for many decisions, users of break-even charts require analysis of changes only in a small "relevant range" of production. Within this range, linear functions may be useful approximations to more complex functions.

VI. *Cash break-even analysis* as illustrated in Figure 4-4 can be used to analyze the firm's situation on a *cash* basis. Although the analysis does not fully represent cash flows, it is useful because it provides a picture of the flow of funds from operations.

A. For the financial manager and for considerations of solvency, the analysis of cash flows is of paramount importance.

B. Some decisions have a greater impact on cash flows than on net income.

1. A firm may capitalize some types of expenses paid in cash. This will have a favorable effect on net income but will nevertheless represent a cash outlay.

2. In comparing alternative forms of financing, the cash outflow requirements of different forms of financing can be substantial. (See balance sheet on sources and uses of funds on p. 33.)

VII. The sources and uses of funds statement indicates on an historical basis where cash came from and how it was used.

A. The sources and uses of funds analysis is an important planning tool. With it the firm is able to respond to the question raised by prospective lenders: "How has the firm used the funds it received in the past?"

B. Sources and uses analysis on a *pro forma* basis is essential for planning, as it

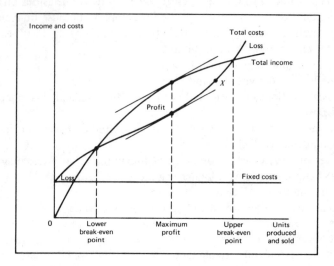

NOTE: The angle of a line from the origin to a point on the total-income line measures price, that is, total income/units sold = price—and a line from the origin to the total-cost curve measures cost per unit. It can be seen that the angle of the line to the revenue curve declines as we move toward higher sales, which means the price is falling. Unit costs (Total cost/Units produced) declines to point X, the tangency point of a line from the origin to the total-cost curve, then begins to rise. The slopes of the total-cost and total-income lines measure marginal cost (MC) and marginal revenue (MR) respectively. At the point where the slopes of the two total curves are equal, $MR = MC$, and profits are at a maximum.

FIGURE 4-3   Nonlinear break-even chart

provides both a plan for the use of funds and, later on, a check to see if the funds were used according to plan.
  C. To construct a rough-and-ready sources and uses statement, tabulate the changes in the balance sheet items from one year to the next and classify them as follows:
   1. *Uses of funds* include (1) increases in asset items or (2) decreases in liability items.
   2. *Sources of funds* include (1) decreases in asset items or (2) increases in liability items.
   3. *Depreciation* is a noncash outlay. Since it is deducted from revenues to determine net income, it is added back as a source of funds.
      A *pro forma,* or projected, sources and uses of funds statement is illustrated below.

Comparative balance sheets and sources and uses of funds
(in millions of dollars)

	12/31/69	Estimated 12/31/70	Sources	Uses
Cash	$ 10	$ 5	$ 5	
Marketable securities	25	15	10	
Net receivables	15	20		$ 5
Inventories	25	30		5
Gross fixed assets	150	180		30
Less: Allowance for depreciation *	(40)	(50)	10	
Net fixed assets	110	130		
Total assets	$185	$200		
Accounts payable	$ 10	$ 6		4
Notes payable	15	10		5
Other current liabilities	10	14	4	
Long-term debt	60	70	10	
Preferred stock	10	10	—	—
Common stock	50	50	—	—
Retained earnings	30	40	10	
Total claims on assets	$185	$200	$49	$49

*The allowance for depreciation is actually a liability account, even though it appears on the left side of the balance sheet. Note that it is deducted, not added, when totaling the column.

Statement of projected sources and uses of funds, 1970
(in millions of dollars)

Uses	Amount	Percent
Gross fixed assets expansion	$30	61.2
Inventory investment	5	10.2
Increase in receivables	5	10.2
Reduction in notes payable	5	10.2
Reduction in accounts payable	4	8.2
Total use of funds	$49	100.0
Sources		
Increase in long-term debt	$10	20.4
Increase in retained earnings	10	20.4
Noncash depreciation outlay	10	20.4
Sale of marketable securities	10	20.4
Reduction in cash holdings	5	10.2
Increase in other liabilities	4	8.2
Total source of funds	$49	100.0

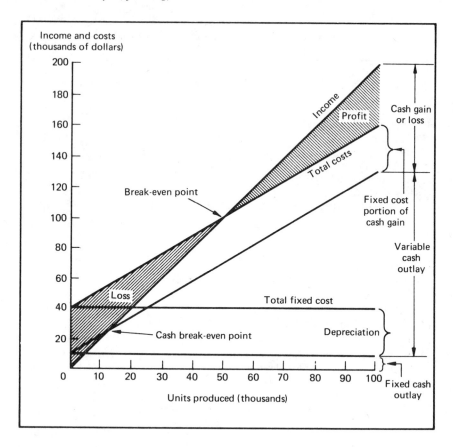

FIGURE 4-4   Cash break-even analysis

4. A brief summary of the illustrative statement may be helpful.
   a. The main *sources* of funds are expected to come from (1) an increase in long-term debt financing, (2) a reduction in holdings of marketable securities, (3) retained earnings, and (4) the noncash depreciation charge.
   b. The major *uses* of funds are expected to be (1) investments in fixed assets, (2) inventories, (3) accounts receivables, and (4) the reduction of a portion of the notes payable.

PROBLEMS

4-1. You are planning to establish a pizza parlor off campus. A graduate business student's market survey of the Westwood area indicates that you could sell 150,000 pizzas at 75 cents apiece. Pizza parlors of this type normally have a 25 percent profit margin before tax. If you require a 15 percent before-tax return on investment, how large an investment should you be willing to make?

Solution:

a. 150,000, pizzas
   <u>   0.75</u>
   $112,500

b. $112,500
   <u>   0.25</u>
   $ 28,125, profit margin before tax

c. $\frac{\$28.125}{0.15}$ = $187,500, maximum investment

4-2. The Mikall Company indicates that the following statement is representative of its operations:

Net sales (1,250,000 units at $4)		$5,000,000
Less: Cost of goods sold		
Materials	$1,000,000	
Labor	1,400,000	
Overhead	<u>1,600,000</u>	<u>4,000,000</u>
Gross profit		$1,000,000
Less: Operating expenses		
Selling expenses	$ 350,000	
Administrative expenses	<u>250,000</u>	<u>600,000</u>
Profit		$ 400,000

Costs and expenses in the income statement are redistributed as follows:

	Total	Variable	Fixed
Materials	$1,000,000	$1,000,000	
Labor	1,400,000	1,400,000	
Factory overhead	1,600,000	400,000	$1,200,000
Selling expenses	350,000	150,000	200,000
Administrative expenses	<u>250,000</u>	<u>50,000</u>	<u>200,000</u>
	$4,600,000	$3,000,000	$1,600,000

a. From the above information, construct a break-even chart in its conventional form and designate areas and points of particular significance.
b. What is Mikall Company's degree of operating leverage at sales of 1,250,000 units?
c. Indicate the special assumptions involved in break-even analysis, as well as any limitations that may be found in such an analysis.

Solution:

a. The following two problems illustrate typical break-even analysis.

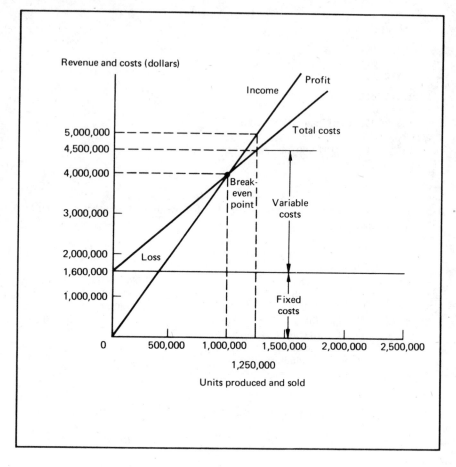

Break-even in terms of units:

$$V = \frac{\$3,000,000}{1,250,000 \text{ units}} = \$2.40 \text{ per unit}$$

$$Q = \frac{F}{P - V} = \frac{\$1,600,000}{\$4.00 - \$2.40} = 1,000,000 \text{ units}$$

Break-even in terms of dollar sales:

$$\text{Break-even point} = \frac{F}{1 - \dfrac{TVC}{\text{Sales}}} = \frac{\$1,600,000}{1 - \dfrac{\$3,000,000}{\$5,000,000}} = \frac{\$1,600,000}{0.4}$$

$$= \$4,000,000$$

b. Degree of operating leverage at point Q =

$$\frac{Q(P - V)}{Q(P - V) - F} = \frac{1,250,000\ (\$4.00 - \$2.40)}{1,250,000\ (\$4.00 - \$2.40) - \$1,600,000}$$

$$= \frac{\$2,000,000}{\$2,000,000 - \$1,600,000} = 5.0$$

c. *Assumptions:*
1. Behavior of costs is reliably determined and linear over the relevant range.
2. Costs can be broken down into fixed and variable categories.
3. Fixed costs remain constant over the volume range on the break-even chart.
4. Variable costs fluctuate with volume.
5. Prices or costs do not change.
6. Efficiency and productivity remain unchanged.
7. Sales mix is constant.
8. All factors are based on a going concern.
9. Beginning and ending inventories are fairly stable.

Limitations:
1. Major limitation is the validity of the assumptions in all the above cases.
2. Static analysis.
3. Break-even analysis disregards the relationship between price and quantity sold.

4-3. Thorp Company sells finance textbooks at $8 each. The variable cost per book is $6. At current annual sales of 800,000 books, the publisher is just breaking even. It is estimated that if the authors' royalties are reduced, the variable cost per book will drop by $1. Assume that the authors' royalties are reduced and that sales remain constant; how much more money can the publisher put into advertising (a fixed cost)?

Solution:

$$
\begin{aligned}
Q &= F/P - V \text{ at break-even } Q \\
Q &= \text{quantity produced} \\
F &= \text{fixed costs} \\
P &= \text{sales price per unit} \\
V &= \text{variable costs per unit}
\end{aligned}
$$

a. 800,000 books $= \dfrac{\text{fixed cost}}{\$8 - \$6}$; fixed cost $= \$1,600,000$

b. 800,000 books $= \dfrac{\text{fixed cost}}{\$8 - \$5}$; fixed cost $= \$2,400,000$

c. $2,400,000
−1,600,000
$ 800,000, difference

4-4. Given the following balance sheet changes, what change, if any, should appear in retained earnings?

$ 3,000 increase in cash
$11,000 increase in inventories
$ 3,000 increase in depreciation
$11,000 increase in accounts payable
$ 6,000 decrease in notes payable

Solution:

Source and uses of funds statement

	Use of funds	*Source of funds*
Cash	3	
Inventories	11	
Depreciation		3
Accounts payable		11
Notes payable	6	
	20	14
Increase in retained earnings		6
	20	20

Theme: In obtaining funds at the lowest interest cost and on the best possible terms, it is important to plan needs far enough in advance to allow sufficient time for effective negotiations. Financial planning makes a great contribution to the efficient performance of the financial manager's responsibilities.

I. The cash flow cycle.

   A. The logic behind financial forecasting is made clear by tracing through the firm's cash flow cycle. Firms need assets in order to make sales, and if sales increase, assets must also grow.

   B. The cash cycle, also called the working capital cycle, shows the process of turning cash into inventories, then into receivables, then back into cash.

   C. This is the sequence of steps.

      1. Original cash investment is used to pay rent and buy equipment.

      2. Raw material purchases are financed by trade credit, giving rise to accounts payable.

      3. Funds are paid to labor to begin processing the raw material.

      4. Before goods are completed, they represent work-in-process inventories. The firm's cash has declined, and current liabilities in the form of accounts payable and accrued wages payable are in existence.

      5. Goods are finished and go from in-process inventories to finished goods inventories. The firm is more liquid at this point because finished goods have salability which work-in-process inventories do not have.

      6. When goods are sold on credit, they become accounts receivable.

      7. Collection of accounts receivable generates cash for the repayment of outside creditors.

      8. The firm buys raw materials, and the working capital cycle, or cash cycle, is repeated.

   D. Rising sales projections call for increases in assets, and funds may be needed to acquire these assets.

      1. Total permanent assets increase in the form of both fixed and current assets.

2. With fluctuations in sales, total assets fluctuate.
3. Permanent assets, both current and fixed, should be financed from long-term sources.
4. Fluctuating asset requirements, or temporary increases in assets, may be financed from short-term sources. This is illustrated in Figure 5-1.

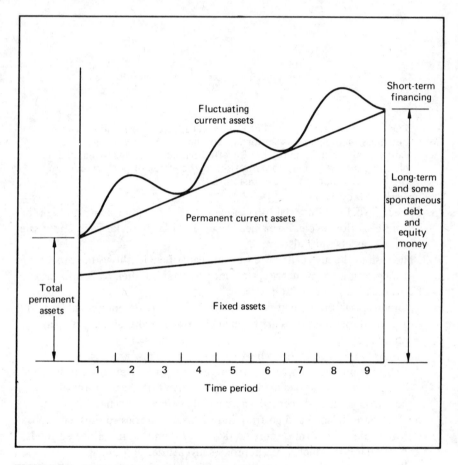

FIGURE 5-1   Fluctuating versus permanent assets

II. Forecasting methodology.
  A. Basic relationships:
    1. To forecast requires the identification of a cause-and-effect relationship. Otherwise, any forecast represents a judgment or a "hunch."
    2. In financial forecasting, sales is the "causal" variable: To make sales, a firm must have both inventories and the equipment used to manufacture or store inventories. When a firm makes sales on credit, these credit sales "cause" accounts receivables to come into existence.

B. Leads and lags necessitate planning.
   1. A firm must have equipment and inventories before making sales. Thus, the need to finance inventories and equipment precedes sales.
   2. Receivables result after sales are made; thus the asset item receivables "lags" sales.
   3. The interaction of these leads and lags gives rise to financial dynamics and the need for effective efforts in both planning and control.
C. These are the basic methods of forecasting:
   1. Percent-of-sales method expresses each item as a percentage of sales. For example, if sales were $1,000,000 and accounts receivable were $200,000, the percent-of-sales relation for accounts receivable would be 20 percent.
   2. The scatter diagram, or regression, method must be used if the relation is such that the proportionality factor changes with the volume of sales (explained below).
III. Percent-of-sales method.
   A. Determine those balance sheet items that vary directly with sales.
   B. Increases in assets represent financing requirements.
   C. Some liabilities grow spontaneously with sales.
   D. The difference between the required growth in assets and the spontaneously generated funds from liability increases represents the firm's financing requirements (before retained earnings).
   E. Table 5-1 provides an illustration.

TABLE 5-1   The Moore Company—Balance sheet items expressed as a percent of sales, December 31, 1970

Cash	2.0%	Accounts payable	10.0%
Receivables	17.0	Accrued taxes and wages	5.0
Inventories	20.0	Mortgage bonds	N.A.
Fixed assets (net)	30.0	Common stock	N.A.
		Retained earnings	N.A.
Total	69.0%	Total	15.0%

Assets as a percent of sales	69.0%
Less: Spontaneous increase in liabilities	15.0
Percent of each additional dollar of sales that must be financed	54.0%

F. *Retained earnings* play an important role.
   1. The increase in retained earnings is unique among all the other balance sheet items that are tied to sales.
   2. While the increase in the other balance sheet items is related to the *increase* in sales, the increase in retained earnings is a percentage of *total* sales.

3. The relation between the percentage increase in sales, the profit margin on sales, and the percentage of incremental sales that requires financing determines the extent of external financing requirements.
   4. An increase in sales gives rise to the following relations:
      a. Assets must increase by 54 percent of the sales increase.
      b. With a profit margin on sales of 5 percent (and no dividends paid), the increase in retained earnings would be 5 percent of *total* sales (not the increase in sales).
      c. In equation form:

$$\text{Financing needed} = (\text{assets percent} - \text{spontaneous liabilities percent}) \times \Delta S - (\text{profit margin}) \times S$$

where ΔS = increase in sales and S = total sales during the forecast year. If growth is slow, then ΔS is small and financing needs are likewise small. If growth is rapid, ΔS is large and so are financial requirements. Thus, the greater the rate of growth, the greater the requirement for external financing.

IV. Scatter diagram or regression method.
   A. Regression analysis develops relationships based on sales as the independent variable (plotted on the horizontal scale) and on the asset item as the dependent variable (plotted on the vertical scale).
   B. Proceed as follows:
      1. Forecast or project the sales of the firm by GNP, industry sales, or other logical business indicators.
      2. Plot the scatter diagrams for major asset, liability, and net worth categories related to sales.
      3. Fit the regression line by freehand (inspection) or by numerical calculations (least squares).
      4. Project the regression lines and determine the level of each balance sheet category for the forecast value of sales.
      5. The difference between total asset requirements and financing sources directly related to sales indicates financial requirements.
V. Comparison of forecasting techniques.
   A. For short-term forecasts, such as month-to-month, either the ratio method or the regression method may be employed.
   B. For longer term forecasts, it is best to use the regression method to avoid major errors that might result from systematic shifts in the ratios.
   C. Table 5-2 and Figure 5-2 illustrate the use of the percent-of-sales method of forecasting financial requirements compared with the regression method.

TABLE 5-2   Relations between inventory and sales

Years	Sales	Inventory	Inventory as a percent of sales
1964	$ 50,000	$22,000	44
1965	100,000	24,000	24
1966	150,000	26,000	17
1967	200,000	28,000	14
1968	250,000	30,000	12
1969	300,000	32,000	11
1972 (estimated)	500,000		

D. The implications of the data in the table and figure can be indicated by first calculating the regression line for the data (The following simplified procedure is applicable when the regression line is a straight line).
  1. First calculate the slope of the line by relating the change in inventory to the change in sales.
    a. When sales increased by $100,000, the increase in inventories was $4,000.
    b. The slope is, therefore,

$$\frac{\text{change in inventories}}{\text{change in sales}} = \frac{\$4,000}{100,000} = .04 = 4 \text{ percent}$$

    c. The intercept of the regression line can be estimated by taking a point on the regression line, using the slope as calculated above, and solving for A in the following equation of a straight line.

$$Y = A + BX$$

    For sales of $250,000, the corresponding inventories in 1968 were $30,000; we know that $B = .04$, so substituting,

$$\$30,000 = A + .04\,(\$250,000)$$
$$\$30,000 = A + \$10,000$$
$$\$20,000 = A$$

    d. The general relationship for the data in Table 5-2 is

$$\text{inventories} = \$20,000 + .04\,(\text{Sales})$$

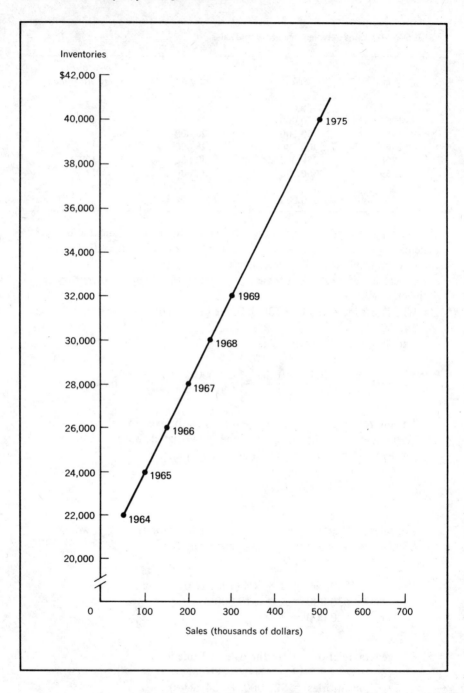

FIGURE 5-2   Illustrative relationship between sales and inventory

2. The intercept term indicates that a $20,000 base stock is held, to which additional amounts of inventories are added as sales change. Mathematically, a nonzero intercept is associated with a *changing* percentage of inventories to sales as shown in the last column of Table 5-2, indicating that the percent-of-sales method would cause faulty forecasting.

3. These are some guidelines for use of the percentage method versus the regression method:

   a. When the regression line has a nonzero intercept, the use of the percentage method for forecasting would involve error.

   b. Since the percentage of inventories-to-sales is declining, the use of any of the percentages in the last column of Table 5-2 for forecasting with a rising sales volume would represent lax standards for control.

   c. In general, the regression method is more dependable as a method for forecasting.

   d. For the present example, the use of the regression method would result in the following forecast of inventories for 1972 when sales are forecast to be $500,000:

$$Inventories = \$20,000 + .04(\$500,000)$$
$$= \$40,000$$

   e. Using the percentage for the latest year, 1969, would result in an inventory projection of .11 ($50,000) = $55,000. This represents an inventory control standard of $15,000 which is too large as compared with the amount determined by the regression method.

4. Either method provides about the same results under two circumstances:

   a. The regression line has a small intercept (close to zero).

   b. For monthly forecasts or other circumstances in which sales do not vary greatly, the percentage method will provide reasonably dependable control estimates.

PROBLEMS

5-1. The Western Corporation's sales were $900,000 in 1970. During 1971, it expects its sales to increase by 50 percent. Total assets were $300,000 in 1970. The same percentage of assets to sales will be maintained in 1971. At the close of 1970, common stock was $150,000 and retained earnings were $80,000. Net profit after taxes is expected to be 8 percent of sales in 1971. No dividends are paid. Assuming the debt on hand as of the close of 1970 is not repaid, what amount of new financing will be needed in 1971?

Solution:

1970
total assets − (stock + retained earnings) = debt
$300,000 − ($150,000 + $80,000) = $70,000
sales = $900,000

$$\frac{\$300,000 \text{ assets}}{\$900,000 \text{ sales}} = 33.3\%$$

1971
sales 1.5 × $900,000 (1971 sales) = $1,350,000 (1971)

$$\frac{\text{assets}}{\text{sales}} = \frac{\text{assets (1971)}}{\$1,350,000} = 33.3\%$$

assets (1967) = $450,000
net profit = 8% × sales = 8% × $1,350,000
   net profit = $108,000

$ 70,000, debt   Note: $ 80,000 (1970)
  150,000, stock   108,000 (profits net 1971)
  188,000, retained earnings $188,000 (1971)
$408,000

$450,000, new asset level (1971)
 408,000, existing financing
$ 42,000, new financing needed in 1971

Alternative solution:

Step 1:   Total sales in 1970 $ 900,000
         Add:
             Increase in sales in 1971 = 0.5($900,000):   450,000
             Total sales in 1971: $1,350,000

Step 2:

$$\frac{\text{Total assets (1970)}}{\text{Total sales (1970)}} = \frac{\text{Total assets (1971)}}{\text{Total sales (1971)}}$$

$$\frac{\$300,000}{\$900,000} = \frac{\text{Total assets (1971)}}{\$1,350,000}$$

Total assets 1971 = $450,000

$$\frac{\text{Total assets (1971)}}{\text{Total sales (1971)}} = \frac{\$450,000}{\$1,350,000} = 33.3\%$$

Step 3: Use the equation form:

$$\text{Financing needed} = \frac{\text{assets as \%}}{\text{of sales}} - \frac{\text{spontaneous liabilities}}{\text{as \% of sales}}$$

$$\times \Delta S - \frac{\text{profit}}{\text{margin}} \times S$$

Where ΔS = increase in sales, and S = total sales during forecast year.

or in our case:

$$\text{Financing needed} = \frac{\text{assets as \%}}{\text{of sales}} \times \Delta S - [\text{profit margin}] \times S$$

$$= [33.3\%] \times \$450,000 - [8\%] \times \$1,350,000$$

$$= \underline{\$42,000}$$

5-2. The Granite Company's sales were $720,000 in 1970, but it expects to double this volume to $1,440,000 during 1971. The net profit after taxes is expected to be 5 percent of sales. Each balance sheet account will have the following percent of sales tied up in it:

Cash	2%
Receivables	6%
Inventory	12%
Fixed assets	5%
Accounts payable	5%

On December 31, 1970, the Common Stock account shows $100,000 and the Retained Earnings $44,000. No dividends are to be paid on common stock during 1971.

a. Complete two balance sheets, one as of December 31, 1970, and the other as of December 31, 1971, using "financing needed" to balance out.
b. Determine "financing needed" by the formula method.
c. What is the significance of your results?

Solution:

a.

Granite Company—Balance sheets, December 31, 1970 and 1971

	1970	1971		1970	1971
Cash	$ 14,400	$ 28,800	Accounts		
Receivables	43,200	86,400	payable	$ 36,000	$ 72,000
Inventory	86,400	172,800	Financing		
Fixed assets	36,000	72,000	needed	—	72,000
	$180,000	$360,000	Common stock	100,000	100,000
			Retained		
			earnings	44,000	116,000
				$180,000	$360,000

Retained earnings during 1971 equal $72,000 (5% of $1,440,000). This amount added to $44,000 gives a retained earning total of $116,000 at the end of 1971.

b.

$$\text{Financing needed} = \frac{\text{assets as \%}}{\text{of sales}} - \frac{\text{spontaneous liabilities}}{\text{as \% of sales}} \times \Delta S$$

$$- \frac{\text{profit}}{\text{margin}} \times S$$

Assets as % of sales = 2% + 6% + 12% + 5% = 25%
Spontaneous liabilities as % of sales = 5%
Financing needed = [25% − 5%] × $720,000 − [5%] × $1,440,000
          = $72,000

c. The practical significance of this problem is that, if a firm is successful and if it grows, it faces increased financing requirements that may not be obtained from internal sources, but must be obtained from external sources.

Note: It should be noted that forecasting by the percent-of-sales method assumes that historical balance sheet and income statement relations are constant. While in fact these relations may be stable in many cases, they often are intended as simplifying assumptions (especially as the time horizon is extended) and should be applied with judgment. Note that in this problem the balance sheet items maintained a stable percentage relation to sales, as sales doubled.

Chapter 6

Financial Planning and Control: Budgeting

Theme: An essential part of the financial manager's role is short-term budgeting, and especially cash forecasting, or cash budgeting. The entire budgeting process is examined in Chapter 6.

I. A budget is a tool for obtaining the most productive and profitable use of the company's resources by improving the firm's internal coordination.

A. Budgets are used for planning purposes, and also for control, by comparing plans with results.

B. Budgets provide management with a continuous monitoring system which allows the firm to anticipate new events and react quickly to change.

C. Budgets are an additional form of communication between top management and divisional personnel.

D. Budgets help to clarify the relationship of the divisions to the totality of the firm.

II. The Process of control is carried out in three steps:

A. Standards of performance are established in advance of actual performance.

B. Performance is evaluated relative to the standards.

C. Corrective action is taken if performance is below standard.

III. Figure 6-1 illustrates budget relations.

IV. Assuming that a sales forecast has been made, the series of budgets follow logically.

A. The production budget is developed to include the following:

1. Beginning and ending inventory requirements.

2. The adjusted cost per unit of goods produced.

3. The number of units produced.

B. The number of units to be produced is the first input for the *materials purchases budget*. This budget derives an estimate of raw materials purchases.

C. Formulation of the *cash budget* relies on elements from previous budgets.

1. The *production budget* provides the following:

a. Sales data, which determine accounts receivable collections and selling expenses.

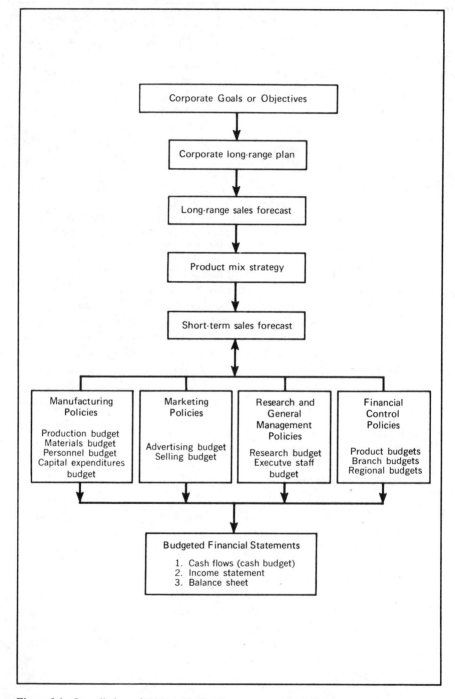

Figure 6-1 Overall view of the total budgeting process and relations

    b. Units produced, which determine direct labor expense and variable manufacturing expense.

  2. The *materials purchases budget* provides the raw materials purchases estimate, which determines the accounts payable payments.

D. The *budgeted income statement* requires the adjusted cost of goods sold figure. This figure is calculated from the following:

    a. Cost of goods produced.

    b. Inventory data in the *materials purchases budget*.

E. Finally, the *budgeted balance sheet* can be derived by the use of information from all the previous budgets.

V. *The Cash Budget.*

A. In a complete budget system, a cash budget performs an important planning and controlling function.

B. The methodology is quite logical.

  1. If a firm sells on credit, there is a lag between sales and cash collections.

  2. Similarly, a firm buying on credit benefits from a waiting period before having to disburse cash.

  3. In expenditures, some cash payments are made in "lumps" at uneven intervals, while expenses may be assigned on a uniform monthly basis.

  4. It is important to take into account debt service requirements, including interest and principal repayment, as outward cash flows.

  5. In general, the cash "throw-off" from operations should meet debt service requirements plus an appropriate margin of safety.

  6. Capital outlays may be covered by specific financing programs.

VI. A *flexible budget* is achieved by varying budget allowances related to sales, by establishing different budgets for different sales volumes, and by supplementing a basic budget by periodic adjustments.

A. The flexible budget utilizes the logic of the regression technique to determine the impact of the control variable (that is, the independent variable) on the item for which a budget figure is to be determined.

B. Knowledge of the firm's operations is required to discover the cause-and-effect relationships and to apply them in a budget system.

VII. The following are suggestions for making budget systems work.

A. Budgeting is often done implicitly in lieu of a formal budget system. *Implicit budgeting* does not bring assumptions into focus and can lead to errors.

B. The choice of a budget period is flexible and should fit the needs of the firm.

C. For the budget system to be of the most value in the control process, a series of charts should be set up. In that way, trends can be most easily observed.

D. The financial manager should avoid common pitfalls in budgeting.

  1. Budgets can become cumbersome.

  2. Budgetary goals can supersede enterprise goals.

  3. Budgets can hide inefficiencies.

4. Budgets can cause inflexibilities.
5. Budgets can be used as instruments of tyranny.
VIII. Financial plans and budgets are used by other departments in addition to finance.
  A. They are used for overall company planning; the personnel department uses them for hiring and training activities; and the production department uses them for planning capacity requirements.
  B. The plans are used in both long-term and short-term decisions.
    1. Long-term decisions:
      a. The regression method is used to plan needs for three to five years.
      b. The sequence and mix of retained earnings, common stock, and debt financing is planned.
    2. Short-term decisions:
      a. The percent-of-sales method is frequently used.
      b. The cash budget is emphasized, indicating how funds will be used and when they will be repaid.
      c. Such information is important in obtaining bank loans.
      d. The full integration between balance sheets, income statements, cash budgets, and other budgets is presented to provide prospective lenders with information indicating that the firm and its financial manager have a full understanding of the business and have developed effective plans, budgets, and controls. The objective is to avoid "surprises" both for management and for its financing sources—to demonstrate that the firm can effectively control its operations according to plans.
IX. An effective financial control system encompasses these areas:
  A. The controls used should be designed to measure deviations from plans. Managers should evaluate controls periodically in order to remove obsolete ones and institute new ones as needed.
  B. Controls must be related to levels of authority, because the one who carries out the control function must be responsible for the performance of the controlled activity.
  C. The cost of controls should be kept consistent with the importance of the item under control.
  D. The acceptance of controls is increased if those who operate under the standards participate in formulating them.
  E. Performance must be measured against standards. Judgment is necessary in the appraisal of performance.
  F. Deficiencies that are revealed by controls must be corrected to complete the feedback system.

PROBLEMS

6-1.   You have been asked to prepare a cash budget for Crystal Stores for the period July 1 through December 31. The following data are provided:

a. All sales are for credit. Payment for 10 percent of the sales is received during the month in which the sales are made, 60 percent in the month following, and 30 percent in the second month following.
b. Purchases during each month equal 75 percent of the following month's sales. Payment for purchases is made in the month following the purchase.
c. Inventory equals a base stock of $8,000 plus purchases for the following month.
d. The firm's minimum level of cash is $5,000. Cash is $6,000 as of July 1.
e. The firm buys no additional fixed assets during the period.
f. Accrued wages and salaries remain unchanged at the end of the period.
g. Borrowings are in the form of notes payable.
h. Other current liabilities remain unchanged at the end of the period.
i. The firm is a corporation that pays no dividends.
j. The gross profit margin is 25 percent.
k. Sales data and wages and salaries data are:

	Actual	
	Sales	*Wages and salaries*
May	$20,000	$2,000
June	20,000	2,000

	Forecast	
	Sales	*Wages and salaries*
July	$30,000	$2,500
August	50,000	3,000
September	50,000	3,000
October	60,000	3,500
November	30,000	3 000
December	20,000	2,000
January	20,000	2,000
February	20,000	2,000

l. Rent is $500 per month, depreciation is $400 per month, and other cash expenses are 2 percent of sales.

Prepare a cash budget for the six-month period.

Solution:

Crystal Stores—Cash budget work sheet

	May	June	July	Aug.	Sept.	Oct.	Nov.	Dec.	Jan.	Feb.
Sales	$20,000	$20,000	$30,000	$50,000	$50,000	$60,000	$30,000	$20,000	$20,000	$20,000
Collections:										
10% (present month)			$ 3,000	$ 5,000	$ 5,000	$ 6,000	$ 3,000	$ 2,000	$ 2,000	$ 2,000
60% (next month)			12,000	18,000	30,000	30,000	36,000	18,000	12,000	12,000
30% (two months later than present month)			6,000	6,000	9,000	15,000	15,000	18,000	9,000	6,000
Total			$21,000	$29,000	$44,000	$51,000	$54,000	$38,000	$23,000	$20,000
Purchases of 75% of next month's sales	$15,000	$22,500	$37,500	$37,500	$45,000	$22,500	$15,000	$15,000		
Payments		15,000	22,500	37,500	37,500	45,000	22,500	15,000	15,000	

Crystal Stores—Cash budget

	July	Aug.	Sept.	Oct.	Nov.	Dec.
Receipts: collections	$21,000	$29,000	$44,000	$51,000	$54,000	$38,000
Payments:						
Purchases	$22,500	$37,500	$37,500	$45,000	$22,500	$15,000
Wages and salaries	2,500	3,000	3,000	3,500	3,000	2,000
Rent	500	500	500	500	500	500
Other (2% sales)	600	1,000	1,000	1,200	600	400
Total payments	$26,100	$42,000	$42,000	$50,200	$26,600	$17,900
Net cash gain (loss)	($ 5,100)	($13,000)	$ 2,000	$ 800	$27,400	$20,100
Initial cash, $6,000						
Cumulative cash	$ 900	($12,100)	($10,100)	($ 9,300)	$18,100	$38,200
Minimum cash desired	5,000	5,000	5,000	5,000	5,000	5,000
Cash above minimum needs (or financing needs)— cumulative minus desired	($ 4,100)	($17,100)	($15,100)	($14,300)	$13,100	$33,200

Part III

Long-Term Investment Decisions: Capital Budgeting

Chapter 7

The Interest Factor
in Financial Decisions

Theme: Most financing decisions involve commitments over extended periods. The interest factor will therefore have a crucial impact on the soundness of the decisions.

I. Compound amount or compound value is defined as the sum (V) to which a beginning amount of principal (P) will grow over n years when interest is earned at the rate of i percent a year.

A. $V = P(1 + i)^n$.

B. Letting IF = (interest factor) = $(1 + i)^n$, the above equation may be written as $V = P(IF)$. It is necessary only to go to an appropriate interest table to find the proper interest factor (Table A-1).

C. The compound value of $1,000.00 at 4 percent for 5 years may be found as $V = \$1,000(1.217) = \$1,217$.

II. *The present value of a future payment* (P) is the amount which, invested at a specified interest rate (i), would equal the future payment (V).

A. Finding present values (or discounting) is simply the reverse of compounding.

B. The present value of $1,217 at 4 percent is found as

$$P = V \ \frac{1}{(1 + i)^n} = \$1,217 \,(0.822) = \$1,000.$$

The term in brackets is called the present value interest factor (IF); $P = V(IF)$. (Table A-2.)

III. An annuity is defined as a series of payments of a fixed amount (R) for a specified number of years. The first payment is assumed to occur at the *end* of the first year. The *compound value of an annuity* is the total amount one would have at the end of the annuity period if each payment was invested at a given interest rate and held to the end of the annuity period.

A. S_n = compound value of an annuity, R = the annual receipt, i = the interest rate, n = the number of years, and

$$S_n = R \frac{(1 + i)^n - 1}{i}$$

$S_n = R(IF)$ where IF is the interest factor shown in brackets directly above. (Table A-3.)[1]

B. Compounded value of a $1,000 annuity invested at 4 percent for 3 years: compound value = $IF \times$ annual receipt = 3.122 $\times$ $1,000 = $3,122.

IV. The *present value of an annuity* is the required lump sum on hand today to permit withdrawals of equal amounts (R) at the end of each year for n years.

A. A_n = the present value of an annuity, R = the annual receipt, and

$$A_n = R \frac{1 - (1 + i)^{-n}}{i}$$

$$A_n = R (IF)$$

B. To withdraw $1,000 a year for 3 years, for example, requires:

$$A_n = R(IF)$$

$$= \$1,000 \times 2.775 = \$2,775$$

V. There are other uses of the basic equations.

A. To determine annual payments required to accumulate a future sum:

1. $R = \dfrac{S_n}{IF}$

2. What amount of money must be deposited at 5 percent for each of the next five years in order to have $10,000 at the end of the fifth year?

$$R = \frac{\$10,000}{5.526} = \$1,810.$$

B. To find the annual receipts from a specified annuity:

1. Beginning with a fixed amount of money, earning a fixed interest rate, you plan to make a series of equal withdrawals. You wish to know the size of the withdrawals that will leave a balance of zero after the last one has been taken.

2. $R = \dfrac{A_n}{IF}$

[1] The equation for an annuity is not derived here.

3. You have $7,000 earning 4 percent interest and you plan to make three equal yearly withdrawals starting in one year.

$$R = \frac{\$7,000}{2.775} = \$2,523$$

C. *Interest rates* may be determined.
1. Frequently one knows the present value and cash flows associated with a payment stream but not the interest rate involved.
2. $IF = \dfrac{V_n}{P}$
3. A bank offers to lend $1,000 today upon agreement to repay $1,217 at the end of five years. What is the rate of interest involved?

$$IF = \frac{1,217}{1,000} = 1.217, \text{ the } IF \text{ for } 4\% \text{ (see Table A-1, 5 years)}.$$

D. To calculate the *present value of a series of uneven annual payments,* use the following formula (subscripts refer to time periods, *X*'s refer to payments):

$$PV = X_1 (IF_1) + X_2 (IF_2) + \ldots\ldots\ldots + X_t (IF_t)$$

E. To calculate the *present value of a payments stream composed of one lump sum plus a stream of equal payments*, use the formula: *PV* = *PV* of lump sum + *PV* of series.
F. *Semiannual and other compounding periods* are often used.
1. Semiannual compounding means that interest is actually paid each six months.
   a. The interest rate is divided by two.
   b. The number of compounding periods is doubled since interest is paid twice a year.
2. The results of more frequent compounding may be calculated also.
   a. Divide the nominal interest rate by the number of times compounding occurs each year.
   b. Multiply the years by the number of compounding periods per year.
3. The general formula for this type of compounding is

$$V_n = P(1 + \frac{i}{m})^{mn}$$

where m = number of compounding periods per year
$\quad\quad n$ = number of years.

VI. How are interest rates determined and evaluated?
  A. The general level of interest rates in the economy is determined by the inter-action of the supply and demand for funds.
    1. Funds are supplied by individuals, corporate savers, and banks, within the overall control of the Federal Reserve System.
    2. Funds are demanded by business, individual borrowers, and government bodies.
  B. The structure of interest rates is determined by the following influences:
    1. The level of risk.
    2. The term or maturity of the debt.
    3. Other characteristics of the borrower.
  C. In evaluating the yields of a prospective investment, one must consider its opportunity costs.
    1. A wide range of alternative potential investments is available in the economy.
    2. An individual relates alternative prospective yields and risks to his needs and attitudes toward the possibility of losses.
    3. A new investment is compared with the best of existing alternatives.
    4. Opportunity cost of investing in a new alternative is the yield on the old alternative, which the new replaces.

PROBLEMS

7-1. At an annual growth rate of 10 percent, how long will it take to triple a sum of money?

Solution: (Refer to the Compound Sum Table) 3.000 appears halfway between the 11th year (2.853) and the 12th year (3.138) in the 10 percent column; it therefore requires about 11.5 years to triple the sum of money.

7-2. If you bought a nondividend paying stock 13 years ago for $34 and the stock is now selling for $97, at what rate of interest has your capital grown?

Solution: (Refer to the Compound Sum Table)
$97/34 = 2.853
2.853 appears in the 13th year at about 8.5 percent

7-3. Which amount is worth more at 8 percent: $2,000 today or $3,500 after five years?

Solution: The *PV* of $3,500 at 8 percent over 5 years is:

PV = $3,500 × 0.681 = $2,384, which is larger than $2,000.

Therefore $3,500 after five years at 8 percent is worth more than $2,000 today.

7-4. Because of illness, your 45-year-old aunt is expected to live only another ten years. You have placed her life savings of $22,000 in a bank earning 8 percent annually. She makes the first withdrawal one year from today. How much can she withdraw at the beginning of each of the remaining years to leave exactly zero in the account at the end of the tenth year?

Solution: (Refer to the Present Value of an Annuity Table)
    Factor for nine years at 8 percent annually is 6.247
    $22,000/6.247 = $3,522

7-5. How much must be invested today, at a 23 percent rate, in order to accumulate $5 in two years? (Credit for this problem will be given only if your answer indicates you have worked it without the use of the interest tables.)

Solution:

$$X (1.23)^2 = \$5$$
$$X (1.51) = 5$$
$$X = 5/1.51 = \$3.31$$

7-6. A savings and loan association advertises a 7 percent rate of interest compounded semiannually. What effective rate of interest is the savings and loan paying?

Solution:

$$(1 + 0.035)^2 - 1 = (1.0712) - 1 = 7.12\%$$

7-7. What amount would an investor be willing to pay for a $1,000, 5-year bond which pays $40 interest semiannually and is sold to yield 6 percent?

Solution:

a. $1,000, maturity value of the bond
    X0.744, present value factor, 3% for 10 semiannual periods
    $ 744

b. $ 40.00 , semiannual interest
    X   8.530, present value of an annuity factor of 3% for 10 semiannual periods
    $341.20

c. $ 744.00
       341.20
    $1,085.20

7-8. The Smith Coal Company is establishing a fund to fill in and replant forests over a strip mine. $700,000 will be required to do the job, and the funds will be needed ten years from now. The company plans to put a fixed amount into the fund each year for ten years, the first payment to be made in one year. Assume the fund will earn 5 percent a year. What annual contribution must be made to accumulate the $700,000 at the end of ten years?

Solution: The answer is found as the sum of an annuity at the end of ten years. Use Table A-3.

$$\text{Annual payment} \times 12.578 = \$700,000$$
$$\text{Annual payment} = \frac{\$700,000}{12.578} = \$55,653 \text{ a year}$$

7-9. Your uncle will lend you $2,000 today if you agree to pay him $2,208 in five years. What rate of interest is your uncle charging you?

Solution:

$$IF = \frac{\$2,208}{\$2,000} = 1.104$$

Looking across the five-year row in Table A-1, we find the *IF* = 1.104 in the 2 percent column. Your uncle is charging you 2 percent interest, which is a good deal today!

Chapter 8

Capital Budgeting Technique

Theme: Capital budgeting is of the greatest significance because it involves commitments for large outlays whose benefits (or drawbacks) extend well into the future.

I. The capital budget is a plan of expenditures for fixed assets. It is significant for these reasons:

  A. It represents a decision whose results continue over an extended period.

  B. It represents an implicit sales forecast. Inaccurate forecasts will result in overinvestment or underinvestment in fixed assets.

  C. Good capital budgeting will improve the timing of asset acquisitions and the quality of assets purchased.

  D. Asset expansion involves substantial expenditures. The requisite financing must be arranged in advance.

  E. Failure occurs both because of too much capital investment and because of undue delay in replacing old equipment with modern equipment.

II. Overall view of capital budgeting is as follows:

  A. It is an application of the classic economic theory that marginal revenue should be equated to marginal cost.

  B. The demand for capital goods is represented by an investment return schedule.

  C. The supply of funds is represented by the firm's marginal cost of capital.

III. Investment proposals are assembled in categories:

  A. Replacements.

    1. Assets wear out and become obsolete.

    2. Estimates of cost savings by purchases of new equipment are reliable.

  B. Expansion investments.

    1. Additional capacity is provided in existing product lines.

    2. Estimates are based on prior experience.

  C. New product activities.

    1. This represents a form of expansion and possibly diversification.

    2. Estimates are subject to a wider margin of error.

IV. Administration of capital budgeting includes the following:
  A. Approvals.
    1. Typically larger dollar amounts require higher levels of approval.
    2. Review and approval of major outlays is an important function of boards of directors.
  B. Planning horizon.
    1. It varies with the nature of the industry.
    2. It is becoming longer as technology advances.
  C. Payment schedule and post-audits.
    1. Finance department works with other departments to compile systematic records on the uses of funds.
    2. Data are also compiled on equipment purchased.
    3. Feedback data on actual savings should be compiled.
    4. Comparisons between earlier estimates and actual data provide a basis for review of past decisions and the formulation of new decisions.
V. Choosing among alternative proposals.
  A. Frequently there are more proposals for projects than the firm is able or willing to finance.
    1. The proposals are ranked.
    2. A cutoff point is determined.
  B. There are two basic types of proposals:
    1. *Mutually exclusive* proposals are alternative methods of performing the same job, such as a choice of conveyor belts versus fork-lift trucks for materials handling.
    2. *Independent items* are capital equipment considered for performing difficult tasks.
  C. Good data is important.
    1. Reliable estimates of cost savings or revenue increases are critical.
    2. Effective record keeping for meaningful post-audits is essential.
    3. Good data require competent individuals to make the estimates.
VI. Three methods for *ranking investment proposals* are described.
  A. The *payback period* is the number of years required to return the original investment. It is conceptually weak, because it ignores income beyond the payback period and does not take into account the fact that a dollar received today is more valuable than a dollar received in the future.
  B. *Internal rate of return* (IRR) is the interest rate that equates the present value of future returns to the investment outlay.
    1. Although it is more difficult to calculate the internal rate of return than the payback, the rate of return method overcomes the conceptual flaws noted in the use of the payback method.
    2. The IRR method recognizes that a dollar received immediately is preferable to a dollar received at some future date.
  C. The *net present value method* (NPV) is the present value of future returns discounted at the cost of capital, minus the cost of the investment.

1. This method meets the objections to the payback method, as does the internal rate of return method.
2. The NPV method is generally preferable for ranking investment proposals.
VII. Calculation procedures.
   A. Estimate the actual cash outlays attributable to the new investment.
   B. Calculate incremental cash inflows.
      1. Depreciation is not deducted.
      2. Depreciation is relevant only for determining tax savings.
   C. Tax savings are an essential part of the analysis.
   D. The present value of cash outflows and cash inflows is calculated.
   E. The internal rate of return is compared with the cost of capital, or a determination is made of the net present value.
   F. Following is an illustrative work sheet for calculations for replacement decisions.

Calculations for replacement decisions

	Amount before tax	Amount after tax	Year event occurs	Present value factor at 10%	Present value
Outflows at time investment is made					
Investment in new					
equipment	10,000	10,000	0	1.00	$10,000
Salvage value of old	(1,000)	(1,000)	0	1.00	(1,000)
Tax loss on sale	(4,000)	(2,000)	0	1.00	(2,000)
Total outflows (present value of costs)					$ 7,000
Inflows, or annual returns					
Benefits*	3,000	1,500	1–10	6.145	9,217
Depreciation on new					
(annual)	1,000	500	1–10	6.145	3,073
Depreciation on old					
(annual)†	(500)	(250)	1–10	6.145	(1,536)
Salvage value on new**	—	—	—	—	—
Total inflows (present value of benefits)					$10,754
Present value of inflows less present value of outflows					$ 3,754

*$1,000 sales increase + $2,000 cost saving = $3,000 benefit.
†Had the replacement not been made, Culver would have had $500 depreciation a year on the old machine—$5,000 book value divided by 10 years. But since they made the replacement, this depreciation is no longer available. The $5,000 has been recovered as $1,000 salvage plus $4,000 deductible loss. The depreciation of $500 a year must, therefore, be subtracted from inflows. It would, of course, have been possible for Culver to not sell the old machine, not take the immediate loss, and continue getting the $500 a year depreciation. However, the present value of this would be only $1,536 versus $3,000 ($2,000 + $1,000) for the sale and tax loss.
**The new machine has a zero estimated salvage value at the time it is purchased. However, the table is structured to show how salvage value would be handled in cases where it is applicable.

VIII. New projects and new product evaluations.
   A. The principles and analysis for replacement decisions, as outlined, are applicable to a wide range of capital asset investment decisions.
   B. The following are some common elements involved in the analysis of capital investment decisions:
      1. The amount and timing of outflows are determined so that they may be discounted back to the present.
      2. The amount and timing of inflows are set so that they may be discounted back to the present.
      3. Tax savings, salvage values, and other cash flows are also considered.
      4. The calculations of net present values (NPV) are made.
IX. The total capital budget is then formulated.
   A. It is necessary to select from a broad range of capital budgeting opportunities, and interrelationships among investment proposals must be noted:
      1. A capital budget is tentatively formulated.
      2. The allocation of corporate funds and decisions as to whether to raise additional funds are ordinarily made by the board of directors, the finance committee, or the executive committee—it is a high level decision.
      3. The capital budgeting program and financing decisions are simultaneously and interactively determined.
   B. A composition problem may arise.
      1. Individual projects may promise attractive yields, but difficulties might be involved in assuming all favorable projects simultaneously.
      2. If other firms in the same industry are expanding capacity or reducing costs, it may be impossible for all the firms to achieve their goals.
   C. The size of the total budget must be determined.
      1. Some firms follow the rule of thumb that growth will be financed only out of internally generated funds.
      2. Maintenance of a constant debt-to-equity ratio causes restricted growth if equity financing is not undertaken.
      3. If there is an absolute limit on the amount of debt financing, expenditures will be cut back in these instances:
         a. Internally generated funds are too small to make up the deficit.
         b. The firm will not undertake equity financing.

PROBLEMS

8-1. As the cost of capital increases without limit, the present value:
   a. Goes to plus infinity.
   b. Stays unchanged.
   c. Goes to zero.
   d. Must have dollar amount of investment to answer.
   e. Goes to minus infinity.

Solution: c. Goes to zero.

8-2. What is one major advantage of the payback method?
a. Explicit consideration of all receipts generated during the life of an investment.
b. Adjustment for the time value of all inflows.
c. Focus on speed of return of invested funds.
d. Discounting of incremental outflows.
e. Focus on cash flows over time.

Solution: c. Focus on speed of return of invested funds.

8-3. A $770 investment has the following cash returns:

Year	
1	$500
2	$125
3	$250

Find the internal rate of return.

Solution:

Cash flow	9% PV factors (from Table A-2)	Discounted cash flow	8% PV factors (from Table A-2)
$500	0.917	458.5	0.926
125	0.842	105.3	0.857
250	0.772	193.0	0.794
		756.8	

Cash flow	Discounted cash flow	7% PV factors (from Table A-2)	Discounted cash flow
$500	463.0	0.935	467.5
125	107.1	0.873	109.1
250	198.5	0.816	204.0
	768.6		780.6

Internal rate of return = approximately 8 percent

8-4. A firm has been presented with an investment opportunity which will yield ten years of increased annual profits as given below. If the cost of the investment is an immediate outlay of $125,000 and the firm requires a 10 percent return on its investment, what is the net present value of the investment? (Ignore taxes.)

Year(s)	Return
1	$80,000
2-9	$25,000
10	$30,000

Solution:

a.

Years	Table	PV factors	Returns	Discounted return
1	A-2	0.909	$80,000	$ 72,720
2-9	A-4	4.850	$25,000	$121,250
10	A-2	0.386	$30,000	$ 11,580

$205,550, present value of future returns

Note: The 2-to-9-year factor can be obtained from Table A-4 by sub-tracting the first-year value from the ninth-year value in the 10 percent column (5.759 − .909 = 4.850).

b. $205,550, present value of future returns
   −125,000, present cost of the investment
   $ 80,550, net present value of the investment

8-5. Each of two projects requires an investment of $800. The firm's cost of capital is 10 percent. The cash flow patterns (income returns after taxes plus depreciation) are as follows:

Year	A	B
1	$400	$100
2	400	200
3	200	200
4	100	200
5		300
6		400

a. Calculate the present value and net present value of each project at each of the following costs of capital: 0, 4, 6, 8, 10, 15, 20 percent.
b. Rank the investments by the following methods:
   1. Payback.
   2. Internal rate of return.
   3. Net present value at cost of capital of 10 percent.
c. Graph the results of part 1 with cost of capital on the horizontal axis and (1) present value on the vertical axis and (2) net present value on the vertical axis.
d. What is the practical significance of your findings in a, b, and c?

Solution:

a. Original investment = $800

Year	A	B
1	400	100
2	400	200
3	200	200
4	100	200
5		300
6		400

Year	Interest factor	0% A	0% B	Interest factor	4% A	4% B	Interest factor	6% A	6% B
1	1.0	400	100	0.962	385	96	0.943	377	94
2	1.0	400	200	0.925	370	185	0.890	356	178
3	1.0	200	200	0.889	178	178	0.840	168	168
4	1.0	100	200	0.885	86	171	0.792	79	158
5	1.0		300	0.822		247	0.747		224
6	1.0		400	0.790		316	0.705		282
Present value		1100	1400		1019	1193		980	1104
Net present value		300	600		219	393		180	304

Year	Interest factor	8% A	8% B	Interest factor	10% A	10% B	Interest factor	15% A	15% B
1	0.926	370	93	0.909	364	91	0.870	348	87
2	0.857	343	171	0.826	330	165	0.756	302	151
3	0.794	159	159	0.751	150	150	0.658	132	132
4	0.735	74	147	0.683	68	137	0.572	57	114
5	0.681		204	0.621		186	0.497		149
6	0.630		252	0.564		226	0.432		173
Present value		946	1026		912	955		839	806
Net present value		146	226		112	155		39	6

Year	Interest factor	20% A	20% B
1	0.833	333	83
2	0.694	278	139
3	0.579	116	116
4	0.482	48	96
5	0.402		121
6	0.335		134
Present value		775	689
Net present value		(25)	(111)

b. 1. Payback period: A, 2 years; B, $4\,{}^1/_3$ years
   A is better than B.
   2. Internal rate of return: A, 18%; B, 15¼%
   A is better than B.
   3. Net present value (at 10% cost of capital)
   A: $112, B: $155
   B is better than A.
c. 1. Present value

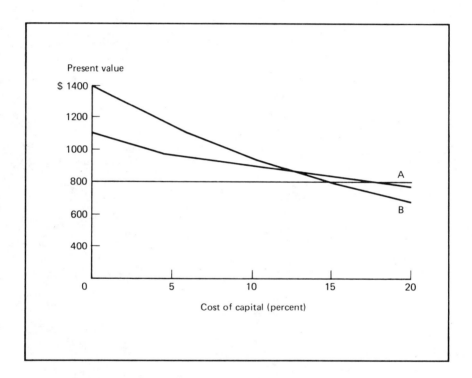

Significance of the findings: (a) The different methods result in different rankings. (b) The payback, average investment, and internal rate of return have the defects indicated in the text. (c) At low costs of capital, project B is better than project A. At high costs of capital, project A is better than project B.

This indicates that projects cannot be ranked without taking the cost of capital into account; otherwise, errors may result.

2. Net present value

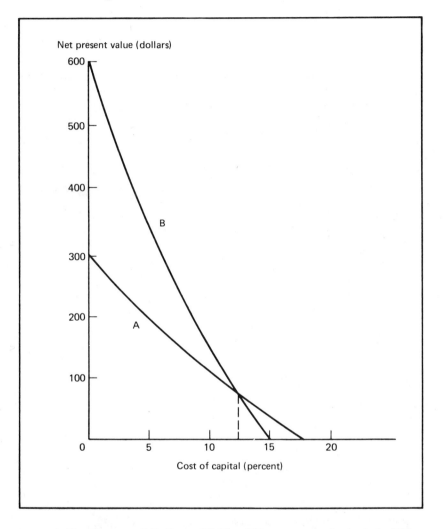

d. Significance of findings: (1) The different methods result in different rankings. (2) The payback has the defects indicated in the text. (3) At a cost of capital of 10 percent, *B* is better than *A*. At a rate of 12½ percent a potential investor should be indifferent between the two investment alternatives. Beyond the internal rates of return (*A*: 18 percent, *B*: 15¼ percent) both investments have negative net present values; thus, it is unlikely that either would be accepted. This indicates that projects cannot be ranked without taking the cost of capital into account; otherwise, errors may result.

It should be apparent that if a firm uses a high cost of capital, it will tend to make short-term investments, and, similarly, long-term investments if a low cost of capital is employed.

8-6. The Eastern Company is using a computer whose original cost was $25,000. The machine is now five years old and has a current market value of $5,000. The computer is being depreciated over a 10-year life toward zero estimated salvage value. Depreciation is on a straight-line basis. Management is contemplating the purchase of a new computer whose cost is $50,000 and whose estimated salvage value is $1,000. Expected savings from the new computer is $3,000 a year. Depreciation is on a straight-line basis over a seven-year life and the cost of capital is 10 percent. Assume a 50 percent tax rate.
a. Should the firm replace the asset?
b. How would your decision be affected if the expected savings from the investment in the new computer increase to $15,000 a year, its salvage value increases to $5,000 but the expected life of the new computer decreases to five years?
c. With regard to the changes in b, how would your decision be affected if a second new computer is available that costs $60,000, has a $6,000 estimated salvage value, and is expected to provide $22,000 in annual savings over its five-year life? Depreciation is still on a straight line basis. Use only the NPV method.
Note: Compare the NPV of replacing the old computer by the second new computer, to the NPV of part b.

Solution:

a.

Outflows at time investment is made	Amount before tax	Amount after tax	Timing	Table	(10%) IF	PV
Investment in new computer	$50,000	$50,000	0	—	1.0	$50,000
Selling price of old computer	(5,000)	(5,000)	0	—	1.0	(5,000)
Tax loss on sale of old computer	(7,500)	(3,750)	0	—	1.0	(3,750)*
Total outflows						$41,250

Inflows, or annual returns	Amount before tax	Amount after tax	Timing	Table	(10%) IF	PV
Savings	$ 3,000	$ 1,500	1-7	A-4	4.868	$ 7,302
Depreciation on new computer	7,000	3,500	1-7	A-4	4.868	17,038
Depreciation on old computer	(2,500)	(1,250)	1-5	A-4	3.791	(4,739)
Salvage value on new computer	1,000	1,000	7	A-2	0.513	513
Total inflows						$ 20,114
NPV						$(21,136)

On the basis of the above analysis, the firm should not replace the asset.

Tax Loss Computation
Straight-line depreciation of a $25,000 machine over ten years yields $2,500 depreciation each year. The machine is five years old and hence has $12,500 remaining book value. Selling it for $5,000 generates a $7,500 before tax loss on the sale ($12,500 − 5,000 = 7,500), $3,750 after tax.

b. Outflows at time investment is made, are the same as in part a: $41,250.

Inflows, or annual returns	Amount before tax	Amount after tax	Timing	Table	(10%) IF	PV
Savings	$15,000	$ 7,500	1-5	A-4	3.791	$28,433
Depreciation on new computer	9,000	4,500	1-5	A-4	3.791	17,060
Depreciation on old computer	(2,500)	(1,250)	1-5	A-4	3.791	(4,739)
Salvage value on new computer	5,000	5,000	5	A-2	0.621	3,105
Total inflows						$43,859
Total outflows						$41,250
NPV						$ 2,609

On the basis of the above analysis, the firm should replace the asset.

c.

Outflows at time investment is made	Amount before tax	Amount after tax	Timing	Table	(10%) IF	PV
Investment in second new computer	$60,000	$60,000	0	−	1.0	$60,000
Selling price of old computer	(5,000)	(5,000)	0	−	1.0	(5,000)
Tax loss on sale of old computer	(7,500)	(3,750)	0	−	1.0	(3,750)
Total outflows						$51,250

Inflows, or annual returns	*Amount before tax*	*Amount after tax*	*Timing*	*Table*	*(10%) IF*	*PV*
Savings	$22,000	$11,000	1-5	A-4	3.791	$41,701
Depreciation on new computer	10,800	5,400	1-5	A-4	3.791	20,471
Depreciation on old computer	(2,500)	(1,250)	1-5	A-4	3.791	(4,739)
Salvage value on new computer	6,000	6,000	5	A-2	0.621	3,726
Total inflows						$61,159
NPV						$ 9,909

NPV (c) > NPV (b)
$9,909 > $2,609

The firm will select to invest in the second new computer.

Chapter 9

Capital Budgeting Under Uncertainty

Theme: The essential elements of risk analysis, and the place of risk analysis in capital budgeting, are presented in this chapter.

I. These are some basic definitions.

A. The *riskiness* of a project is defined in terms of the likely variability of expected future returns on the project.

B. *Variation of expected future returns* is used as a measure of risk.

1. In a normal distribution of rates of return on a set of projects, *the mean return is defined as the expected return,* and *the standard deviation (σ) is used as a measurement of risk.*

a. All other things the same, the higher the expected return, the more attractive the project.

b. The higher the standard deviation, the greater the variability of returns and, by definition, the greater the riskiness of the project.

2. Figure 9-1 illustrates the distribution of probable returns from investments *A* and *B.*

3. One may compare the riskiness of Projects *A* and *B.*

a. Expected returns for *A* and *B* both equal $3,000.

b. Project *A* has a standard deviation of $200, and *B* has a standard deviation of $1,000.

c. Investment *A* is defined to be less risky than investment *B.*

II. Riskiness over time.

A. Visualize investments *A* and *B* in Figure 9-1 as expected cash flows from the same project but in different years.

1. The expected return is the same for both years.

2. The subjectively estimated standard deviation is larger for the more distant return. Riskiness is *increasing over time.*

B. If risk were thought of as being constant over time, then the standard deviation would be constant. This is not generally the case; usually distant returns are more risky, as illustrated in Figure 9-2.

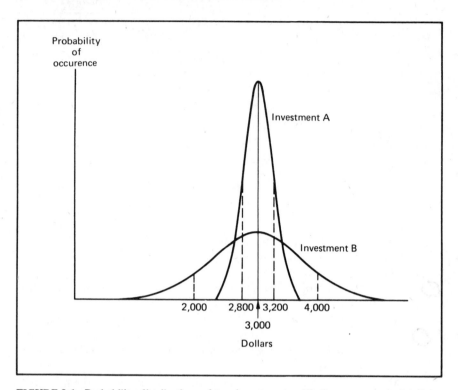

FIGURE 9-1   Probability distributions of two investments with the same expected dollar return

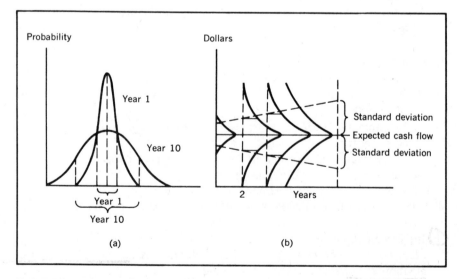

FIGURE 9-2   Risk as a function of time

III. Portfolio effects.
  A. If the returns from a number of projects in which the firm invests are not
     all determined by the same factors, changing economic conditions affect
     the returns from the projects differently. Thus, the size of variations from
     expected returns may be reduced by investing in a number of different types
     of projects, or *portfolios* of projects.
  B. Effects of investment in diversified projects on portfolio risk:
     1. If perfectly negatively correlated projects are available in sufficient num-
        ber, then diversification can completely eliminate risk. Perfect negative
        correlation is, however, almost never found in the real world.
     2. If uncorrelated projects are available in sufficient number, then diversifi-
        cation can reduce risk significantly—to zero at the limit.
     3. If all alternative projects are perfectly positively correlated, then diversifi-
        cation does not reduce risk at all.
  C. Portfolio risks.
     1. When considering the riskiness of a particular investment, it is frequently
        useful to consider the relationship between the investment in question and
        other existing assets or potential investment opportunities.
     2. If there is a high positive correlation between the new project and the firm's
        other assets, the overall risk is not reduced significantly by diversification.
        A correlation of +1.0 results in no risk reduction.
     3. Uncorrelated projects benefit the firm to some extent. If an asset's returns
        are not closely related to the firm's other major assets, this asset is more
        valuable to a risk-averting firm than is a similar asset whose returns are
        positively correlated with the bulk of the assets.
IV. Alternative methods of treating risk.
  A. *Informal treatment.*
     1. For example, the net present values based on single-valued estimates of
        annual returns (using the firm's cost of capital) might be calculated.
     2. If the net present values of two mutually exclusive projects are "reason-
        ably" close to one another, the "less risky" one is chosen. The decision
        rules are strictly internal to the decision-maker.
     3. To formalize the approach, the mean expectation and the standard devi-
        ation of the net PV's may be presented to the decision-maker. However,
        the decision is still made in an unspecified manner.
  B. *The risk-adjusted discount rate.*
     1. The process of choosing among risky assets can be formalized by using
        higher discount rates for more risky projects.
     2. When the risk-adjusted discount rate approach is employed, different dis-
        count rates are prescribed for the various divisions. Divisions then differ-
        entiate among the types of investments by the investments' individual
        riskiness.

3. Risk adjustments should reflect both the estimated standard deviation (or coefficient of variation) of expected returns and investors' attitudes toward risk, as well as portfolio effects.

V. These are advantages for both management and stockholders in corporate diversification.

  A. Since stockholders can diversify investments among different firms, it would be unnecessary for managers to consider diversification of the firm's capital projects under the following conditions:

    1. Perfect capital markets.

    2. No income taxes.

    3. No frictions in expanding and contracting business organizations.

    4. No bankruptcy costs, including money costs and the stigma attached to business failure.

  B. Managements are concerned with corporate diversification for these reasons:

    1. Bankruptcy resulting from the failure of a firm is costly to investors and injures the reputations of managers.

    2. Potential managers would avoid firms where risks of failure were high because of lack of diversification.

    3. Tax laws favor losses by a *division* of a firm versus a separate firm.

  C. Portfolio theory, therefore, remains an important aspect of capital budgeting decisions from the standpoint of the managers of a firm.

    1. Diversification reduces the risks of failure of the firm.

    2. Reducing the risks of failure lowers or eliminates the costs of reorganization and bankruptcy to investors, as well as saving taxes in the aggregate.

PROBLEMS

9-1 In relation to two-product diversification, the *least* beneficial effect of diversification is achieved if the correlation between the two projects is:

  a. +1.0

  b. +0.5

  c.   0

  d. −0.5

  e. −1.0

Solution:

  a. +1.0. If any two projects are perfectly positively correlated, then diversification does nothing to eliminate risk.

9-2 The probability distribution of cash flows from a project with relatively high risk is:

a. A vertical line extending up from the expected value.

b. A horizontal line.

c. Relatively peaked.
d. Relatively flat.
e. Skewed to the left.

Solution:

d. Relatively flat. The flatter the probability distribution of expected future returns, or alternatively stated, the less peaked the distribution, the higher the risk on a project.

9-3. The Mansfield Company is faced with two mutually exclusive investment projects. Each project costs $4,000 and has an expected life of four years. Annual net cash flows from each project begin one year after the initial investment is made and have the following characteristics:

	Probability	*Cash flow*
Project *A*	.1	$2,000
	.4	3,000
	.2	3,600
	.3	3,400
	1.0	
Project *B*	.1	$ 100
	.4	3,500
	.2	7,500
	.3	6,500
	1.0	

Mansfield has decided to evaluate the riskier project at a 12 percent cost of capital versus 9 percent for the less risky project.
a. What is the expected value of the annual net cash flows from each project?
b. What is the risk-adjusted NPV of each project?

Solution:

a. Expected annual cash flow (A) = $2,000 × 0.1 + $3,000 × 0.4
$\qquad\qquad$ + $3,600 × 0.2 + $3,400 × 0.3
$\qquad\qquad$ = $3,140

$\quad$ Expected annual cash flow (B) = $100 × 0.1 + $3,500 × 0.4
$\qquad\qquad$ + $7,500 × 0.2 + $6,500 × 0.3
$\qquad\qquad$ = $4,860

b. Project B is the riskier project because it has the greater variability in its expected cash flows. Hence, project B is evaluated at the 12 percent cost of capital, while project A requires only 9 percent cost of capital.

$$\text{NPV } (A) = \$3,140 \text{ (IF, 9\%, 4 year annuity)} - \$4,000$$
$$= \$3,140 \text{ (3.240)} - \$4,000$$
$$= \$10,174 - \$4,000 = \underline{\underline{\$6,174}}$$

$$\text{NPV } (B) = \$4,860 \text{ (IF, 12\%, 4 year annuity)} - \$4,000$$
$$= \$4,860 \text{ (3.037)} - \$4,000$$
$$= \$14,760 - \$4,000 = \underline{\underline{\$10,760}}$$

The above calculations indicate that Mansfield Company should accept project B in spite of its higher risk.

9-4. The Morton Products Co., Inc., is considering replacing a 15-year-old machine that has a book value of $5,000 and a current market value of $10,000. It is looking at two mutually exclusive alternatives:
1. Replacement with a similar new machine with a $70,000 cost and before-tax cash flows of $22,000 a year. The tax rate is 50 percent.
2. Replacement with a new type of machine, previously untried by either the company or its competitors, for sale by its inventor for $120,000. The expected net cash flows with the new machine are $40,000 a year.
   The first machine has an expected salvage value of $4,000 at the end of its 15-year life, and the new machine has an expected salvage value of $2,000 at the end of its 15-year life. Net depreciation benefits for both machines are included in the calculations of net cash flows above. The firm's cost of capital is 12 percent.
   a. Should the firm replace the existing machine, and if so, should replacement be with a similar new machine or with the new type of machine?
   b. How would your results be affected if a risk-adjusted discount rate of 14 percent were used for the new type of machine?

Solution:

a.

Outflows	Amount before tax	Amount after tax	Timing	Table	(12%) IF	PV
Investment 1	$ 70,000	$ 70,000	0	—	1.0	$ 70,000
Selling price of old equipment	(10,000)	(10,000)	0	—	1.0	(10,000)
Tax on recaptured depreciation	5,000	2,500	0	—	1.0	2,500
Total outflows						$ 62,500

Inflows	Amount before tax	Amount after tax	Timing	Table	(12%) IF	PV
Net cash flows	$ 22,000	$ 11,000	1-15	A-4	6.811	$ 74,921
Salvage value	4,000	4,000	15	A-2	0.183	732
Total inflows						$ 75,653
NPV						$ 13,153

Outflows	Amount before tax	Amount after tax	Timing	Table	(12%) IF	PV
Investment 2	$120,000	$120,000	0	–	1.0	$120,000
Selling price of old equipment	(10,000)	(10,000)	0	–	1.0	(10,000)
Tax on recaptured depreciation	5,000	2,500	0	–	1.0	2,500
Total outflows						$112,500

Inflows						
Net cash flows	$ 40,000	$ 20,000	1-15	A-4	6.811	$136,220
Salvage value	2,000	2,000	15	A-2	0.183	366
Total inflows						$136,586
NPV						$ 24,086

On the basis of the above analysis, the firm should replace with the new machine.

b. Outflows for investment 2 are the same under either discount rate, since all outflows occur in year 0. Hence, costs remain $112,500.

Inflows	Amount after tax	Timing	Table	IF	PV
Net cash flows	$20,000	1-15	A-4	6.142	$122,840
Salvage value	2,000	15	A-2	0.140	280
Total inflows					$123,120

NPV = $123,120 − $112,500 = $10,620

At the higher discount rate, the new process appears less profitable ($10,620 < $13,153), thus replacement is made with a machine similar to the old one.

Part IV

Valuation and Financial Structure

Chapter 10

Financial Structure
and the Use of Leverage

Theme: The purpose of this chapter is to formulate a sound basis
for determining the effect of its financial structure on the firm's cost
of capital.

I. These are some basic definitions.

  A. *Asset structure* is the left-hand side of the balance sheet (the firm's assets
which must be financed).

  B. *Financial structure* is the right-hand side of the balance sheet (the sources
of financing).

  C. *Capital structure* is the permanent financing of the firm, represented by
long-term debt plus preferred stock and net worth (total assets less current
liabilities).

  D. *Financial leverage* is the ratio of total debt to total assets. (Leverage is also
measured by the ratio of total debt to net worth; this ratio is referred to as
the debt-equity ratio.)

  E. *Business risk* is the inherent variability of expected returns on the firm's
"portfolio" of assets.

  F. *Financial risk* is additional risk to common stock resulting from the use of
financial leverage.

II. The theory of financial leverage is presented.

  A. If the return on assets exceeds the cost of debt, leverage is successful. Leverage may increase the returns to equity, but risk is also increased.

  B. Leverage increases returns to owners if successful, and decreases the returns
to owners if unsuccessful.

  C. At some degree of leverage the cost of debt rises because of increased risk
with the higher fixed charges.

  D. Risks of increased debt also affect the holders of common stock, causing
expected returns on common stock to rise.

III. The procedure for calculating the comparative costs of alternative forms of
financing is explained.

  A. Here are the steps in the procedure:

1. Begin with the present level of sales; determine the earnings per share. From the observed current market price of the stock, the current price-to-earnings ratio can be determined.
2. Estimate the increased investment required for the projected potential sales increase.
3. Estimate net income and earnings per share at various levels of sales and for each form of financing.
4. Capitalize the earnings per share. (At some leverage ratio, applicable capitalization rates will begin to rise because of the greater risk involved. This point is covered in some depth in Chapter 11.)
5. Make break-even charts of earnings per share and capitalized earnings per share.
6. These break-even charts suggest the relative costs of alternative combinations of financing.

B. Table 10-1 illustrates the procedure.
   1. These are the basic assumptions of the example:
      Sales are currently $2,000,000. It is estimated that by an additional investment of $1,000,000, sales could be increased to $4,000,000. But the industry is subject to fluctuations in demand, so the level of sales could also be as low as $500,000. The firm has no interest-bearing debt at present. The current price-earnings ratio is 15. If the additional financing is obtained through debt, the cost of debt will be 10 percent and the price/earnings ratio will drop to 14. The new stock could be sold at $50 per share. If the additional financing is obtained through the sale of equity, the cost of debt will be 7 percent and the price-earnings ratio will rise to 16.
      Fixed costs are $500,000 and variable costs are 40 percent of sales. The tax rate is 50 percent. There is no debt outstanding at present.
   2. Analysis of relations

TABLE 10-1   Universal Machine Company—Comparative costs of alternative forms of financing

a. Before additional investment

Units sold	50,000	100,000	200,000	300,000	400,000
Selling price per unit	$10	$10	$10	$10	$10
Sales	$500,000	$1,000,000	$2,000,000	$3,000,000	$4,000,000
Fixed costs	500,000	500,000	500,000	500,000	500,000
Variable costs	200,000	400,000	800,000	1,200,000	1,600,000
Total costs, except interest	$700,000	$ 900,000	$1,300,000	$1,700,000	$2,100,000

TABLE 10-1   (continued)

Earnings before interest and taxes	$(200,000)	100,000	700,000	1,300,000	1,900,000
Taxes*	(100,000)	50,000	350,000	Inadequate capacity	
Earnings after taxes	(100,000)	50,000	350,000	for sales over	
Earnings per share on 100,000				$2,000,000	
shares	$(1.00)	$0.50	$3.50		
Market price per share (P/E = 15)	—	$7.50	$52.50		

b. Financing with debt

Earnings before interest and taxes	$(200,000)	100,000	700,000	1,300,000	1,900,000
Less: interest	100,000	100,000	100,000	100,000	100,000
Earnings before taxes	(300,000)	–0–	600,000	1,200,000	1,800,000
Less: income taxes	(150,000)	–0–	300,000	600,000	900,000
Net profit after taxes	$(150,000)	–0–	300,000	600,000	900,000
Earnings per share on 100,000 shares	$(1.50)	–0–	$3.00	$6.00	$9.00
Market price per share (P/E = 14)	—	—	$42.00	$84.00	$126.00

c. Financing with common stock

Earnings before taxes†	$(200,000)	100,000	700,000	1,300,000	1,900,000
Less: income taxes	(100,000)	50,000	350,000	650,000	950,000
Net profit after taxes	(100,000)	50,000	350,000	650,000	950,000
Earnings per share on 120,000 shares	$(.83)	$0.42	$2.92	$5.42	$7.92
Market price per share (P/E = 16)	—	$6.72	$46.72	$86.92	$127.00

*Assumes tax credit on losses.
†Earnings before tax is the same as earnings before interest and tax because with no debt the interest cost is zero.
d = deficit, indeterminate

3. Comments on Table 10-1:
   a. While the illustration is based on specific assumptions, the principles are general and could be expressed in general relations.
   b. If sales did not increase, the original situation without the additional financing would produce the greatest earnings per share and the highest indicated market price per share.
   c. If product demand increases expansion of capacity would be required to benefit from the sales opportunities available.
   d. For sales less than $3,000,000, the firm's earnings per share are lower if financing is with debt than if financing is with equity.
   e. Because of the depressed price-earnings ratio and the increased cost of debt, the market price per share is higher for equity financing until the highest sales volume–$4,000,000–is reached.
   f. This method of analysis demonstrates the conditions under which the cost of debt is higher or lower than the cost of equity, but it does not provide a measure of the costs. Calculation of the costs of debt and equity are set forth in Chapters 11 and 12.

IV. Financial leverage is related to operating leverage:
   A. Note that in the illustration in Table 10-1 the results were influenced by both operating and financial leverage.
   B. Both operating and financial leverage have similar effects on profits, and a greater use of either has these results:
      1. The break-even point is raised.
      2. The impact of a change in the level of sales on profits is magnified.
   C. Operating and financial leverage have reinforcing effects:
      1. Operating, or *first stage,* leverage affects earnings before interest and taxes.
      2. Financial, or *second stage,* leverage affects earnings after interest and taxes.
   D. *The degree of operating leverage* was defined in Chapter 4 as the percentage change in operating profits associated with a given percentage change in sales volume:

$$\text{Degree of operating leverage at point } Q = \frac{Q(P - V)}{Q(P - V) - F} \qquad (4\text{-}1)$$

For the data from Table 10-1 at the $2,000,000 sales volume, leverage

$$= \frac{1,200,000}{1,200,000 - 500,000} = 1.71$$

Here Q is units of output, P is the average sales price per unit of output, V is the variable cost per unit, and F is total fixed costs.

E. The degree of financial leverage

The degree of financial leverage is defined as the percentage change in earnings available to common stockholders that is associated with a given percentage change in earnings before interest and taxes (EBIT). An equation has been developed to aid in calculating the degree of financial leverage for any given level of EBIT and interest charges (I):

$$\text{Degree of Financial Leverage} = \frac{Q(P - V) - F}{Q(P - V) - F - I} = \frac{\text{EBIT}}{\text{EBIT} - I} \quad (10\text{-}1)$$

Using the data from Table 10-1 at the $2,000,000 sales volume,

1. Leverage with no additional financing $= \dfrac{700,000}{700,000} = 1.00$

2. Leverage with debt $= \dfrac{700,000}{600,000} = 1.17$

3. Leverage with equity $= \dfrac{700,000}{700,000} = 1.00$

F. Combining operating and financial leverage

Equation (4-1) for the degree of operating leverage can be combined with Equation (10-1) for financial leverage to show the total leveraging effect of a given change in sales on earnings per share:

$$\text{Combined leverage effect} = \frac{Q(P - V)}{Q(P - V) - F - I} \quad (10\text{-}2)$$

For the data from Table 10-1 at the $2,000,000 sales volume

a. No additional financing $= \dfrac{1,200,000}{1,200,000 - 500,000} = 1.71.$

b. Financing with debt $= \dfrac{1,200,000}{1,200,000 - 500,000 - 100,000} = 2.00.$

c. Financing with equity $= \dfrac{1,200,000}{1,200,000 - 500,000} = 1.71.$

V. Among the factors influencing financial structure are these:
A. Growth rate of future sales.
B. Stability of future sales.
C. Competitive structure of the industry.
D. Asset structure of the industry.
E. Control position of owners and management attitudes toward risk.
F. Lender attitudes toward the firm and the industry.
VI. Detailed study of financial ratios among different industries and among firms in the same industry reveals considerable range of variation. However, in firms in the same industry there is a tendency toward a clustering of financial structures.

Reference levels for financial structures

	Percentage of total assets					
	Current liabilities	*Long-term debt*	*Pre-ferred stock*	*Common equity or net worth*	*Cur-rent ratio*	*Times interest earned*
Large, established firms						
Manufacturing	20-25%	15-20%	0-4%	55-65%	2X	8X
Utilities	5-10	45-50	10-15	30-35	1	4
Trade	30-35	16-18	0-2	50-55	2.5	7
Small, rapidly growing, profitable firms						
Manufacturing	40-45%	0-5%	1-10%	40-60%	1X	9X
Trade	50-60	0-5	0-5	30-40	1.5	10

VII. Financial ratio composites may be used in determining the financial plan.
   A. From the averages of financial ratios of firms in a given line of business, a firm can develop a *pro forma* balance sheet.
   B. To construct the *pro forma* financial plan, only two kinds of information are necessary.
      1. The industry of the firm.
      2. An estimate of the firm's annual sales.
   C. The use of financial ratio composites as a guideline can be questioned because the ratio composites are an average in which there is a wide variation among individual firms.
   D. If used, the financial ratio composites should be used as a starting point only.

PROBLEMS

10-1. A firm has a debt ratio of 75 percent. If it has total assets of $200 million, how much can these assets drop in value before creditors are unprotected?

Solution (amounts in millions):

a.
$200, assets $150, debt
$200   50, equity
                  $200

b. $\frac{\$150, \text{debt}}{\$200, \text{assets}}$ = 75%

c. $200
   −150
   $ 50

10-2. The leverage factors of firms A and B are 67 percent and 33 percent respectively. Each firm has $300 million assets and each pays a 6 percent interest rate on debt. Firm A earns 10 percent on assets before interest and taxes; what does it earn on common stock after taxes? What rate of return (before interest and taxes) must firm B earn on its assets if it earns the same rate on common stock after taxes as A? (Assume a 50 percent corporate tax rate.)

Solution (dollar amounts in millions):

	Firm A		Firm B	
Debt	0.67%	$200	0.33%	$100
Equity	0.33	100	0.67	200
Assets	1.00%	$300	1.00%	$300

A earns $300 (0.10)	=	$30
Less: Debt $200 (0.06)	=	12
Taxable income	=	18
Less: Taxes	=	9
Net income	=	$ 9

Rate of return to common stock = $9/$100 = 9%

B's net income $200 (0.09)	=	$18
Plus: Taxes (0.50)	=	18
Taxable income	=	36
Plus: Debt $100 (0.06)	=	6
		$42
Rate of return to assets	=	$42/$300 = 14%

10-3. One useful test or guide for evaluating a firm's financial structure in relation to its industry is by comparison with financial ratio composites for its industry. A new firm or one contemplating entering a new industry may use such industry composites as a guide to what its financial position is likely to approximate after the initial settling-down period.

Bismark Furniture Designs estimates its sales during 1972 as $1,400,000. The following data represent the ratios for the furniture manufacturing industry for 1972:

Sales to net worth	5 times
Current debt to net worth	55%
Total debt to net worth	75%
Current ratio	2.5 times
Net sales to inventory	10 times
Average collection period	42 days
Fixed assets to net worth	48.5%

Bismark Furniture Designs—*Pro forma* **balance sheet, 1972**

Cash	$_____	Current debt	$_____
Accounts receivable	_____	Long-term debt	_____
Inventory	_____	Total debt	_____
Current assets	_____	Net worth	_____
Fixed assets	_____		
Total assets	$_____	Total claims	$_____

Complete the above *pro forma* balance sheet. (Round to nearest thousands.)

Solution:

1. Net worth = sales ÷ net worth turnover = $\dfrac{\$1,400,000}{5}$ = $280,000.

2. Total debt = 75% of net worth = $280,000 × 75% = $210,000.

3. Current debt = 55% of net worth $280,000 × 55% = $154,000.

4. Long-term debt = total debt − current debt = $210,000 − $154,000 = $56,000.

5. Total claims on assets = net worth + total debt = $280,000 + $210,000 = $490,000.

6. Current assets = current debt × current ratio = $154,000 × 2.5 = $354,000.

7. Inventory = sales ÷ inventory turnover = $\dfrac{\$1,400,000}{10}$ = $140,000.

8. Accounts receivable = average collection period × sales per day = $\dfrac{1,400,000}{360} \times \dfrac{42}{1}$ = $163,000.

9. Cash = current assets − (receivables + inventory) = $354,000 − ($163,000 + $140,000) = $51,000.

10. Fixed assets = net worth × 48.5% = $280,000 × 48.5% = $136,000.

11. Total assets = current assets + fixed assets = $354,000 + $136,000 = $490,000.

Bismark Furniture Designs—*Pro forma* **balance sheet, 1972**

Cash	$ 51,000	Current debt	$154,000
Accounts receivables	163,000	Long-term debt	56,000
Inventory	140,000		
Total current assets	$354,000	Total debt	$210,000
Fixed assets	136,000	Net worth	280,000
Total assets	$490,000	Total claims	$490,000

10.4 The Karalus Company wants to double its current capacity in anticipation of increasing market demand. New financing alternatives are:

a. Common stock to net $60 per share (The price-earnings ratio will be 25 times if stock financing is used).

b. Straight 8 percent debt (The price-earnings ratio will be 20 times if stock financing is used).

Current balance sheet

		Debt (4%)	$20,000
		Common stock ($10 par)	30,000
		Surplus	10,000
Total assets	$60,000	Total claims	$60,000

Assume that income, before interest and taxes, is 12 percent of anticipated sales and that the tax rate is 50 percent.

a. What are the expected market prices at sales assumptions of $100,000, $500,000, and $1,000,000 under the two financing alternatives?

b. Make break-even charts for earnings per share and market value per share for the company under the two financing alternatives.

c. At sales volume of $500,000, find (1) the degree of operating leverage, (2) the degree of financial leverage, and (3) the degree of combined leverage effect, under the following three alternatives:

        a. No additional financing.

        b. Debt financing.

        c. Common stock financing.

Assume the following relationships hold at this sales volume:

Average sales price per unit of output = P =	$10.00
Variable cost per unit of output	= V =	$4.00
Total fixed costs	= F =	$240,000.00
Units of output	= Q =	50,000.00

Solution:

a.

Debt financing

	$100,000	$500,000	$1,000,000
Sales	$100,000	$500,000	$1,000,000
Income before interest and taxes (12% X sales)	12,000	60,000	120,000
Interest (4% X $20,000) (8% X $60,000)	5,600	5,600	5,600
Taxable Income	$ 6,400	$ 54,400	$ 114,400
Less: Income Tax (50%)	3,200	27,200	57,200
Net profit after taxes	$ 3,200	$ 27,200	$ 57,200
Earnings per share (3,000 shares outstanding)	$ 1.07	$ 9.07	$ 19.07
Market price*	$ 21.40	$ 181.40	$ 381.40

Common stock financing

Sales	$100,000	$500,000	$1,000,000
Income before interest and taxes	12,000	60,000	120,000
Interest (4% × $20,000)	800	800	800
Taxable income	$ 11,200	$ 59,200	$ 119,200
Less: Income tax (50%)	5,600	29,600	59,600
Net profit after taxes	$ 5,600	$ 29,600	$ 59,600
Earnings per share $\left[\dfrac{\begin{array}{c}3,000\\ +1,000\end{array}}{4,000 \text{ shares outstanding}}\right]$	$ 1.40	$ 7.40	$ 14.90
Market price*	$ 35.00	$ 185.00	$ 372.50

*Market price = Earning per share × [price-earning ratio].

b. Break-even chart for financing alternatives

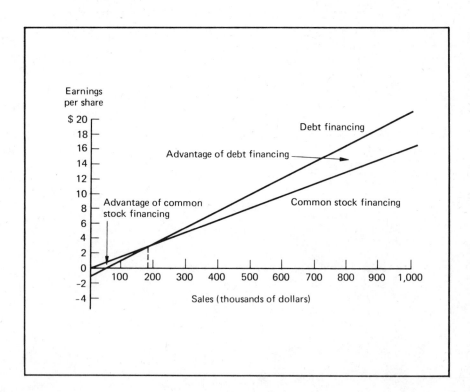

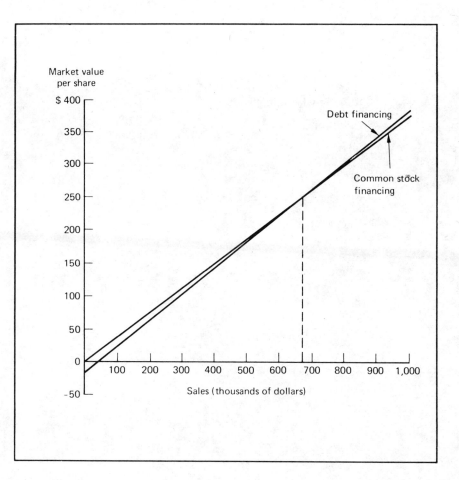

c. 1. Degree of operating leverage at point of $500,000 sales volume =

$$\frac{Q\,(P-V)}{Q(P-V)-F} = \frac{50{,}000\,(\$6.00)}{50{,}000\,(\$6.00)-\$240{,}000} = \frac{\$300{,}000}{\$60{,}000} = 5.00$$

2. Degree of financial leverage $= \dfrac{Q(P-V)-F}{Q(P-V)-F-I} = \dfrac{\text{EBIT}}{\text{EBIT}-I}$

At $500,000 sales volume:

a. No additional financing $= \dfrac{\$60{,}000}{\$60{,}000-\$800} = \dfrac{\$60{,}000}{\$59{,}200} = 1.01$

b. Debt financing $= \dfrac{\$60{,}000}{\$60{,}000-\$5{,}600} = \dfrac{\$60{,}000}{\$54{,}400} = 1.10$

c. Common stock financing $= \dfrac{\$60,000}{\$60,000 - \$800} = \dfrac{\$60,000}{\$59,200} = 1.01$

3. Combined leverage effect $= \dfrac{Q(P - V)}{Q(P - V) - F - I}$

At \$500,000 sales volume:

a. No additional financing $= \dfrac{\$300,000}{\$300,000 - \$240,000 - \$800} =$

$\dfrac{\$300,000}{\$59,200} = 5.07 *$

b. Debt financing $= \dfrac{\$300,000}{\$300,000 - \$240,000 - \$5,600} =$

$\dfrac{\$300,000}{\$54,400} = 5.51 *$

c. Common stock financing $= \dfrac{\$300,000}{\$300,000 - \$240,000 - \$800} =$

$\dfrac{\$300,000}{\$59,200} = 5.07 *$

---

* The combined leverage effect is equal to degree of operating leverage times degree of financial leverage. The numbers shown here are slightly different because of rounding errors.

Theme: The basic principles underlying valuation theory and investors' return on capital are discussed in Chapter 11.

I. There are several definitions of valuation.

  A. *Intrinsic value* is the capitalization of prospective net income flows or net revenues from assets.

  B. *Liquidating value* is the amounts realizable if assets are sold separately from the organization that has been using them.

  C. *Going concern* value is the amount realizable if an enterprise is sold as an operating business.

  D. *Book value* is the accounting value at which an asset is carried.

  E. *Market value* is the price at which an asset (or firm) can be sold.

II. The capitalization of income method of valuation.

  A. This procedure, which is equivalent to the present value of a stream of earnings, is used to determine an asset's intrinsic value.

  B. It has application in bond valuation:

    1. Expected cash flows are the annual interest payments plus the principal amount to be paid when the bond matures.

    2. Capitalization rates applied to bonds vary with differences in risk of default.

    3. The procedure is illustrated for a bond with no maturity (a perpetuity):

$$\text{Value} = V = \frac{\text{constant annual receipts}}{\text{capitalization rate}} = \frac{R}{i}$$

Assume that the annual receipts (R) are $80 and that the going capitalization rate (i) for this type of bond is 8 percent:

$$V = \frac{\$80}{.08} = \$1,000$$

If the capitalization rate rises to 10 percent, the value of the bond will fall:

$$V = \frac{\$80}{.10} = \$800$$

If the capitalization rate falls to 5 percent, the value of the bond will rise:

$$V = \frac{\$80}{.05} = \$1,600$$

4. Illustrations of effect of interest rate changes on bonds with different maturities are given below:

a. Calculation of the value of a five-year bond at different interest rates:

Year	Receipts	Discount factor			Present value of receipts at indicated discount rates		
		8%	10%	5%	8%	10%	5%
1	$80	.926	.909	.952	$74	$73	$76
2	80	.857	.826	.907	69	66	73
3	80	.794	.751	.864	64	60	69
4	80	.735	.683	.823	59	55	66
5	80 + $1,000	.681	.621	.784	735	671	847
Value of Bond					$1,000	$925	$1,131

b. Calculation of the value of a one-year bond at different interest rates

Year	Receipts	Discount factor			Present value of receipts at indicated discount rate		
		8%	10%	5%	8%	10%	5%
1	$80 + $1,000	.926	.909	.952	$1,000	$982	$1,028
Value of Bond					$1,000	$982	$1,028

c. Change in the value of a $1,000 bond with an 8 percent coupon when interest rates change:

	Decline in value as interest rate rises from 8% to 10%	Increase in value as interest rate falls from 8% to 5%
One-year bond	$18	$28
5-year bond	$75	$131
Consol (perpetuity)	$200	$600

C. *Preferred stock valuation*
  1. Most preferred stocks assure their owners regular fixed dividend payments.
  2. Their valuation, therefore, is similar to bond valuation.
III. *Common stock valuation*
  A. There are major differences in debt and preferred stock valuation versus
     common stock valuation:
    1. Income, or receipts, from common stock are subject to greater fluctua-
       tions and more uncertainty.
    2. Common stock earnings and dividends are expected to exhibit growth
       over time, not stay constant, so annuity formulas cannot be used.
  B. The following is a basic stock valuation formula:
    1. Total return = dividend yield + capital gains yield

$$= \frac{\text{expected dividend}}{\text{current price}} + \frac{\text{expected increase in price}}{\text{current price}}$$

    2. An illustration is given.
      a. Assume that the ACO stock has a current market price of $40. It is
         earning $3.60 per share and paying $2.00 a year in dividends. In recent
         years dividends, earnings, and the price of the company's stock have
         been growing 4 percent per year, and they are expected to continue to
         grow at this rate in the future.
      b. The expected return (k) on ACO's stock may be calculated:

$$\text{Present price} = \frac{\text{dividend}}{(1 + k)} + \frac{\text{price in 1 year}}{(1 + k)}$$

$$\text{Present price} = \frac{\text{dividend}}{(1 + k)} + \frac{\text{present price} \times (1 + \text{growth rate})}{(1 + k)}$$

$$\$40 = \frac{\$2.00}{(1 + k)} + \frac{\$40(1.04)}{(1 + k)}$$

$$\$40 = \frac{\$2.00}{(1 + k)} + \frac{\$41.60}{(1 + k)} = \frac{\$43.60}{(1 + k)}$$

$$1 + k = \frac{\$43.60}{\$40.00} = 1.090$$

$$k = 1.090 - 1.00 = 0.090, \text{ or } 9\%$$

      c. The expected rate of return, k, represents two components
        1. dividend yield $= \dfrac{\text{dividends}}{\text{current price}} = \dfrac{\$2}{\$40} = 0.05$, or 5%
        2. capital gains yield $= \dfrac{\text{price increase}}{\text{current price}} = \dfrac{\$1.60}{\$40.00} = 0.04$, or 4%

d. An alternative expression of the above is:

$$k = \text{rate of return} = \frac{D}{P} + g = 5\% + 4\% = 9\%$$

where k = rate of return
D = current dividend
P = current price of the stock
g = expected constant growth rate

e. The following are critical assumptions in the calculations.
1. The profitability rate on new investments will result in a continued earnings growth rate of 4 percent per year.
2. The dividends will remain a constant proportion of earnings, so dividends will also grow at a 4 percent rate.
3. The common stock will also grow at a 4 percent rate, rising as earnings and dividends rise.

IV. The following factors lead to variations in returns among securities.
A. *Risk*
1. This is the most important factor leading to differential expected rates of return.
2. Risk is defined as uncertainty about the return that will actually be realized.
3. Investors as a group dislike risk and, therefore, are "risk averters."
4. If investors are risk averters on the average, greater risk is associated with higher average returns.

B. *Marketability*
1. The higher the liquidity, or marketability, the lower an investment's required rate of return.
2. Listed stocks tend to sell on a lower yield basis than over-the-counter stocks.
3. Publicly owned stocks sell at lower yields than stocks with no established market.
4. Investments in small firms generally require higher yields.

C. *Changes in stock price levels*
1. Its basic influence is determined by conditions of supply and demand.
2. Stock prices are changed by the following:
a. Changes in required rates of return.
b. Changes in growth expectations.
V. *Historical rates of return.*

A. *Ranges of equity yields* for different kinds of firms under varying market conditions are shown below:

Estimated rates of return on common stocks

	Stock market conditions		
	High	*Normal*	*Low*
Company characteristics			
Low risk, high marketability	6½	7	9½
Average risk and marketability	7–8	8–10	12–15
High risk, low marketability	9	12	20

B. Debt yields.
1. Debt yields vary directly with the degree of tightness in money market conditions.
2. Interest rates decline as the size of the loan increases because of the fixed · costs of making and servicing loans.
3. Small loans are made mostly to small firms, and small firms are inherently more risky than large ones.

PROBLEMS

11-1 a. In 1971 the RST Corporation earned $20 million after taxes and paid a $2 quarterly dividend plus an extra dividend of $1.50 at the end of the year. Its current price is $80 a share. Its dividend yield is _____ .

Solution:

$ 8.00, four quarterly $2 dividends
   1.50, extra $1.50 dividend
$ 9.50, total annual dividend

$$\frac{\$ 9.50}{\$80.00} = 11.9\% \text{ dividend yield}$$

b. Assuming four million shares are authorized, and two million shares are outstanding, the RST price-earnings ratio is:

Solution:

$$\frac{\$20,000,000}{2,000,000} = \$10 \text{ EPS}$$

$$\frac{\$80 \text{ price}}{\$10 \text{ EPS}} = 8 \text{ times} = \text{price-earnings ratio.}$$

11-2 The LMN Corporation had the following pattern of earnings during the period 1966-1971

1966	$500,000	1969	$900,000
1967	$700,000	1970	$400,000
1968	$800,000	1971	$200,000

Assuming that future earnings will be equal to the average of past earnings and that an appropriate capitalization rate is 10 percent, estimate the value of LMN on the basis of the capitalization-of-income method of valuation.

Solution:

a.

Year	Earnings
1966	$ 500,000
1967	700,000
1968	800,000
1969	900,000
1970	400,000
1971	200,000
	$3,500,000

b. $3,500,000 total expected earnings/6years = $583,333 average expected earnings.

c. $583,333 average expected earnings/0.10 capitalization rate = $5,833,330 value.

11-3 A stockholder pays $34.50 for a share of stock which he plans to hold indefinitely. If he expects the firm to pay an annual $2.50 dividend and to experience an annual 6 percent stock price appreciation from reinvestment of retained earnings, what will be the rate of return on his original investment? (Use formula given in the text.)

Solution:

$$k = D/P + g$$
$$= 2.50/34.50 + 0.06$$
$$= 0.0724 + 0.06$$
$$= 0.1324 \approx 13.24 \text{ percent}$$

11-4 A firm's stock is currently selling for $40 a share. The firm is earning $4 a share and pays a $3 dividend.

a At what rate must earnings, dividends, and stock price all grow if investors require a 10 percent rate of return? (Use the formula given in the text.)

Solution:

k = $D/p + g$
0.10 = $\$3/\$40 + g$
0.10 = $0.075 + g$
g = 0.025 = 2.5 percent

Alternative solution:

Po = $D_1/(1 + k) + P_1/(1 + k)$
$\$40$ = $\$3/(1.10) + \$40(1 + g)/(1.10)$
$\$44$ = $\$43 + 40g$
$\$1$ = $40g$
g = $1/40$ = 0.025 = 2.5 percent

b. The expected rate of return, 10 percent, can be split into two components—the dividend yield and the capital gains yield. They are respectively:

Solution:

$\dfrac{\$3 \text{ dividend}}{\$40 \text{ price}}$ = 0.075 = 7.5 percent dividend yield

$\$41$, price next year
-40, price this year
$\$\ 1$, capital gain

$\$1/\$40$ = 0.025 = 2.5 percent capital gains yield

c. If the firm reinvests its retained earnings to yield the expected rate of return, what will happen to earnings per share?

Solution:

$\$\quad 4$, EPS
$\underline{-3}$, DPS
$\$\quad 1$, retained earnings per share
$\underline{\times\ 0.10}$, rate of return
$+\$0.10$, increase in EPS

Which is $0.10/4.00$ = 0.025 = 2.5 percent

11-5. a. The bonds of the Academy Corporation are perpetuities bearing an 8 percent coupon and rated AAA. Bonds of this type yield 7 percent. What is the price of Academy bonds? Their par value is $1,000.

b. Interest rate levels rise to the point where such bonds now yield 10 percent. What will be the price of the Academy bonds now?

c. Interest rate levels drop to 8 percent. At what price will the Academy bonds sell?

d. How would your answer to parts a, b, and c change if the bonds had a definite maturity date of 30 years?

Solution:

$1,000 bond with 8 percent coupon rate:
$1,000 × 0.08 = $80, interest per year

a. $\dfrac{\$80}{0.07} = \$1,143$

b. $\dfrac{\$80}{0.10} = \$800$

c. $\dfrac{\$80}{0.08} = \$1,000$ or par

d. 1.
$80 × 12.409* = $ 993
$1,000 × 0.131** = 131
$1,124, smaller than $1,143 (a)

2.
$80 × 9.427* = $ 754
$1,000 × 0.057** = 57
$ 811, larger than $800 (b)

3.
$80 × 11.258* = $ 901
$1,000 × 0.099** = 99
$1,000, the same as $1,000 (c)

11-6. The Westside Company, a small electric car manufacturer, is planning to sell an issue of common stock to the public for the first time. It faces the problem of setting an appropriate price on the stock. The company feels that the proper procedure is to select a firm similar to it with publicly traded shares and to make relevant comparisons. The company learns that Electro, Inc., is similar to it with respect to (1) product mix, (2) size, (3) asset composition, and (4) debt equity proportions.

*Present value of an annuity for $1 for 30 years discounted at 7, 10, and 8 percent (Table A-4).
**Present value of $1, 20 years from today discounted at 7, 10, and 8 percent (Table A-2).

Relation for 1971	Electro	Westside
Earnings per share	$ 2.50	$ 500,000
Price per share	37.50	—
Dividends per share	1.50	250,000
Book value per share	30.00	6,000,000

a. How would these relations be used in guiding Westside in arriving at a market price for the stock?

b. What price would you recommend if Westside sells 300,000 shares?

Solution:

a. As a first step to obtain the boundaries for a final decision, the indicated market price for Westside, compute the per share data:

Earnings per share, 1971	$ 1.67
Dividends per share, 1971	0.83
Book value per share, 1971	20.00

Next, obtain the relevant multiples from the Electro example. The market prices of Electro are the following multiples:

Multiple of earnings per share, 1971	15
Multiple of dividends per share, 1971	25
Multiple of book value per share, 1971	1.25

Now apply the multiples to the Westside data to obtain indicated market prices:

	Indicated market price for Westside stock based on data of Electro
Based on earnings, 1971	$25.05
Based on dividends, 1971	20.75
Based on book value, 1971	25.00

b. The range is between $20.75 and $25.05 a share. Factors tending toward a high range: (a) Westside has had a good recent trend in sales earnings and relative stability of earnings; (b) stock market conditions are favorable; (c) Westside is a company whose product activities are attractive to investors. Factors tending toward a low range are the opposite of factors tending toward a high range.

The actual price would be negotiated between Westside and the underwriter. It should be noted that in making an actual valuation of this kind, it is important to include data both for several years and for several similar firms to avoid basing the price on atypical data.

Chapter 12

The Cost of Capital

Theme: Valuation concepts are applied to develop a weighted cost of capital for the firm.

I. Costs of the individual components of the capital structure.

   A. The *cost of debt* is defined as the interest rate that must be paid on new increments of debt capital, less the tax reduction effect.

   B. The cost of *preferred stock* is the effective yield as measured by the annual preferred dividend, divided by the net price the company receives when it sells new preferred stock.

  C. Taxes have an influence.

    1. Interest payments on debt are deductible; preferred and common stock dividends are not deductible for tax purposes.

    2. Adjust by putting all costs on an after-tax basis.

    3. The after-tax cost of debt equals interest rate times (1-tax rate).

  D. *Cost of equity.*

    1. *Retained earnings.*

      a. The minimum rate of return that must be earned on equity-financed investments to keep unchanged the value of the existing common stock.

      b. This minimum rate of return is that return which investors expect to receive on the company's common stock.

      c. Investors' expectations are greatly influenced by returns they have received in the past.

      d. The cost of retained earnings can be estimated by the formula $k = D/P + g$.

    2. The cost of new outside equity equals the required rate of return on existing common stock divided by (1 − percentage cost of floating new common stock).

II. *The weighted cost of capital.*

  A. These are the first steps:

    1. Determine the costs of individual capital components.

    2. Determine the proper set of weights to use in the calculation process.

B. The optimum capital structure is determined.
  1. This varies from industry to industry.
  2. Management's existing choice of capital structure may be used as a starting point.

C. Should book weights or market weights be used?
  1. Theoretically, market yields and the market value capital structure should be employed.
  2. For marginal increments of capital, book and market values should not differ greatly.
  3. As a practical matter, it appears that firms generally use book values.
  4. Thus, for practical reasons, book weights are likely to be employed.

D. Illustrations of the calculation:
  1. This is the initial set of relations:
    The Burly Company has total net assets of $75 million. It plans to increase net assets to $105 million during the year. Its present capital structure, considered to be optimal, is shown below:

Debt (6% coupon bonds)	$25,000,000	33 1/3%
Preferred stock (8%)	25,000,000	33 1/3%
Equity ($k = 10\%$)	25,000,000	33 1/3%
	$75,000,000	100%

  2. Weighted average cost of capital (historical cost) for initial conditions before addition to capital:

Item	Amount	Cost	Cost Amount
Debt	25,000,000 X 0.03		750,000
Preferred Stock	25,000,000 X 0.08		2,000,000
Common	25,000,000 X 0.10		2,500,000
			5,250,000 ÷ 75,000,000 = 7.00%

  3. Financing the additional $30,000,000 creates the following situation:
    a. Assume that new bonds will have a 7 percent coupon rate and will sell at par. $100 par value preferred will have a coupon rate of 9 percent and will net Burly $90 per share after flotation costs. Common stock, currently selling at $50 a share, can be sold to net the company $45 a share after flotation costs. Stockholders' required rate of return is estimated to be 10 percent. It also is estimated that retained earnings will be $10 million, which will be available and used to meet part of the financing required. The same capital structure will be maintained. The marginal corporate tax rate is 50 percent.

b. Calculations of component costs are as follows:

Cost of debt = (coupon rate) × (1-tax rate) = .07 × .50 = 3.5%.
Cost of preferred stock = 0.09/(1 − .1) = 10.0%.
Cost of retained earnings = 10.0%.
Cost of new outside equity = .10/(1 − .1) = 11.1%.

c. The average cost of capital for the new financing is:

	Cost	Weight	Product
Debt	0.035 ×	0.333 =	0.0117
Preferred	0.100 ×	0.333 =	0.0333
Common	0.100 ×	0.333 =	0.0333

$$0.0783 = 7.83\%, \text{ weighted marginal cost of capital}$$

d. Here is an alternative calculation of weighted marginal cost of capital:

Total cost of financing after $30,000,000 addition:	$7,600,000
Total cost of financing before $30,000,000 addition:	5,250,000
Increment in the total cost of financing:	$2,350,000

$$\frac{\text{Incremental cost}}{\text{Incremental funds}} = \frac{\$ 2,350,000}{\$30,000,000} = 7.83\%$$

4. The weighted cost of new capital if retained earnings had been only $6 million instead of $10 million is:
   a. Cost of equity:

Retained earnings = 10.0%
External equity = 0.110 = .10/(1 − .1) = 11.1%

b. Calculations

	Weights			Cost		Product
Debt	10	0.333	×	0.035	=	0.0117
Preferred	10	0.333	×	0.100	=	0.0333
Retained earnings	6	0.200	×	0.100	=	0.0200
External equity	4	0.133	×	0.111	=	0.0148
	30					0.0798 = 7.98%

c. This again represents the average cost of new capital. The higher cost of the segment of equity funds raised externally causes the average cost of new capital to rise from 7.83 percent to 7.98 percent.

III. The average and marginal costs of capital.
A. The difference is portrayed graphically in Figure 12-1.

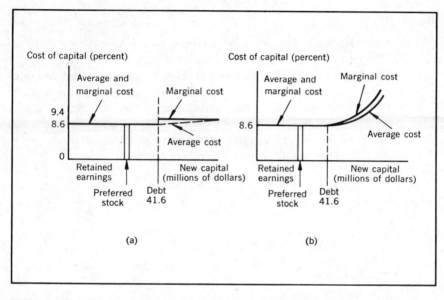

FIGURE 12-1   **Relation between the marginal cost of capital and the amount of funds raised**

B. Marginal cost of capital.
  1. It is the cost of each additional dollar raised during some unit of time, usually a year.
  2. It is used as an investment hurdle rate in capital budgeting.
  3. Net present values must be positive when cash flows are evaluated at the marginal cost of capital.
  4. For a given period of time, usually a year, until internal cash flows have been exhausted, the marginal cost of capital is constant and equal to the average cost of capital.
  5. When external funds must be raised, the marginal cost of capital rises and is greater than the average cost of capital.
C. Average cost of new capital.
  1. It is the average costs of the funds raised during the year.
  2. In planning its capital structure, the firm seeks to minimize the average cost of capital.

3. The average cost of capital is constant until internal equity funds and the debt and preferred stock supported by this equity have been fully utilized.
4. As external equity funds are utilized, the average cost of capital rises but is less than the marginal cost of capital.

PROBLEMS

12-1. Universal Machines, Inc., is currently earning $4 a share, paying a $3.40 dividend, and selling at $42 a share. The company's earnings, dividends, and stock price have all been growing at about 2½ percent a year, and this growth rate is expected to continue indefinitely. According to the firm's investment bankers, a new common stock issue at this time could be sold to net $40.40.

a. Using one of the equations given in the text, calculate Universal's cost of retained earnings (as its required rate of return).

Solution:

$$
\begin{aligned}
k &= D/P + g \\
&= \$3.40/\$42 + 0.025 \\
&= 0.08095 + 0.02500 \\
&= 0.10595 \\
&= 10.595\%
\end{aligned}
$$

Alternative solution:

$$P = \frac{D_1}{1 + k} + \frac{P_1}{1 + k}$$

$$\$42 = \frac{\$3.40}{1 + k} + \frac{42(1.025)}{1 + k}$$

$$1 + k = \frac{\$3.40}{42} + \frac{42(1.025)}{42}$$

$$
\begin{aligned}
1 + k &= 0.08095 + 1.02500 \\
k &= 1.10595 - 1.0 \\
&= 10.595\%
\end{aligned}
$$

b. Using one of the equations given in the text, calculate the price of the stock at the end of one year if the firm's retained earnings are reinvested to yield 2¼ percent rather than the cost of capital. (Assume this new growth rate is expected to be permanent.)

Solution:

1. Calculate the new EPS:

   $4.00 - $3.40 = $0.60, retained EPS

   $0.60 × 0.0225 = $0.014, incremental EPS

   4.00
   0.014
   $4.014, new EPS

2. Calculate the actual growth rate:

   $\frac{$4.014}{4.000}$ = 1.0035; g = 1.0035 - 1.0000 = 0.0035 = .35%

3. Use either formula to obtain the new price:

   a. $P = \dfrac{D}{k - g} = \dfrac{$3.40}{1.10595 - 1.0035}$

   $= \dfrac{$3.40}{0.10245} = 33.19

   b. $P = \dfrac{D}{1 + k} + \dfrac{P(1 + g)}{1 + k}$

   $P = \dfrac{3.40}{1.10595} + \dfrac{P(1.0035)}{1.10595}$

   $P = 33.19

   Notice the big decline in stock price, from $42 to $33.19, caused by the reduced rate of growth.

c. If, when it learned of the reduced return on reinvested earnings, the firm had retained *none* of its earnings (had paid a $4 dividend) and hence had a zero rate of growth, what rate of return would stock-holders receive? (Use the original stock price in your calculation.)

Solution:

$$k = D/P + g = $4/42 + 0 = 0.0952 = 9.52\%$$

d. What is the percentage cost of Universal's newly issued common stock? (Use the required rate of return as calculated in *a*.)

Solution:

1. Required rate of return = 10.595% = k

2. % flotation costs $= \dfrac{\$1.60}{\$42.00} = 0.03809 = 3.809\%$

3. $k_e = \dfrac{k}{1 - \% \text{ flotation cost}} = \dfrac{10.595}{1 - 0.03809} = \dfrac{10.595}{0.96191} = 11.01\%$

12-2. Baker Enterprises has total net assets of $75 million. It plans to increase net assets to $105 million during the year. Its present capital structure, considered to be optimal, is:

Debt (3% coupon bonds)	$25,000,000	33 $\frac{1}{3}$%
Preferred stock	25,000,000	33 $\frac{1}{3}$%
Net worth	25,000,000	33 $\frac{1}{3}$%
	$75,000,000	100%

New bonds will have a 6 percent coupon rate and will sell at par. $100 par value preferred will have a 7 percent rate and will also be sold at par. Common stock, currently selling at $50 a share, can be sold to net the company $45 a share after flotation costs. Stockholders' required rate of return is estimated to be 10 percent. It is estimated that retained earnings will be $4 million. The marginal corporate tax rate is 50 percent.

a. To maintain the present capital structure, how much of the capital budget must be financed by common equity?

Solution:

1. $\dfrac{\$25,000,000}{\$75,000,000 \text{ total liabilities and capital}} = \frac{1}{3}$

2. $30,000,000 capital budget $\times \frac{1}{3} = \$10,000,000$, new equity needed.

b. How much of the new equity funds must be generated externally?

Solution:

$10,000,000 new equity needed
−4,000,000 retained earnings
$ 6,000,000 external equity needed

c. Calculate the cost of retained earnings and new (external) equity:

Solution:

Cost of retained earnings $= k = 10\%$

$$\text{Cost of new equity} = k_e = \frac{k}{1 - \% \text{ of flotation costs}} = \frac{0.10}{1 - \dfrac{\$5}{\$50}}$$

$$= \frac{0.10}{0.90} = 11.11\%$$

d. Compute the weighted average cost of equity.

Solution:

	Amount	Percent	X Cost	= Product
New equity	$ 6,000,000	60	11.11%	0.0666
Retained earnings	4,000,000	40	10.00%	0.0400
Total equity needed	$10,000,000	100		
Weighted average cost of equity				0.1066 = 10.66%

e. Compute the weighted average cost of capital from Baker Enterprise for funds raised during the year.

Solution:

	Percent	X	After-tax cost	=	Product
Debt	33⅓		3.00%		0.00999
Preferred stock	33⅓		7.00%		0.02333
Equity	33⅓		10.66%		0.03553
	100				
Weighted average cost of capital					0.06885 = 6.885%

f. Compute the marginal cost of capital for Baker Enterprises (that is, the cost of the last dollar raised):

Solution:

	Percent	X	After-tax cost	=	Product
Debt	33⅓		3.00%		0.00999
Preferred stock	33⅓		7.00%		0.02333
New common stock (k_e)	33⅓		11.11%		0.03827
	100				
Marginal cost of capital					0.07159 = 7.159%

g. Compute the weighted average cost of capital for Baker Enterprise for funds raised during the year, now assuming retained earnings = $10 million.

Solution:

	Amount	Percent	X	After-tax cost	=	Product
Debt	$10 million	$33\frac{1}{3}$		3.00%		0.00999
Preferred stock	10 million	$33\frac{1}{3}$		7.00%		0.02333
Retained earnings (k)	10 million	$33\frac{1}{3}$		10.00%		0.03333
Capital budget	$30 million	100				
Weighted average cost of capital						0.06665 = 6.665%

h. Compute the marginal cost of capital for Baker Enterprise under the assumption in g.

Solution:

	Percent	X	After-tax cost	=	Product
Debt	$33\frac{1}{3}$		3.00%		0.00999
Preferred stock	$33\frac{1}{3}$		7.00%		0.02333
Retained earnings (k)	$33\frac{1}{3}$		10.00%		0.03333
	100				
Marginal cost of capital					0.06665 = 6.665%

12-3. The Davis Manufacturing Company has the following capital structure as of December 31, 1972:

Debt (7%)		$ 40,000,000
Preferred (8%)		20,000,000
Common stock	$15,000,000	
Retained earnings	25,000,000	
Equity		40,000,000
Total capitalization		$100,000,000

Earnings per share have grown steadily from $1.52 in 1965 to $2.60 estimated for 1972. The investment community, expecting this growth to continue, applies a price-earnings ratio of 25 to yield a current market

price of $65.00. Davis is paying a current annual dividend of $2.60 and it
expects the dividend to grow at the same rate as earnings. The addition to
retained earnings for 1972 is projected at $4 million; these funds will be
available during the next budget year. Assume a 50 percent corporate tax
rate.

Assuming that the capital structure relations set out above are maintained, new securities can be sold at the following costs:

Bonds:	Up to and including $4.0 million of new bonds – 8% yield to investor. From $4.01 to $12 million of new bonds – 9% yield to investor. Over $12 million of new bonds –10% yield to investor.
Preferred:	Up to and including $2.0 million of pref. stock – 9% yield to investor. From $2.01 to $6 million of preferred stock –10% yield to investor. Over $6 million of preferred stock –11% yield to investor.

Common:	Up to $8 million of new outside common stock
	        flotation cost per share = $65 – $60 = $5
	Over $8 million of new outside common stock
	        flotation cost per share = $65 – $55 = $10

a. Compute the average and marginal costs of new capital for asset expansion levels of (a) $10 million, (b) $30 million, and (c) $50 million.
b. Graph the average and marginal costs of capital.

Solution:

a. Step 1. Calculation of weights:

	Amount	*% of total*
Debt	$ 40,000,000	.40
Preferred	20,000,000	.20
Equity	40,000,000	.40
	$100,000,000	1.00

Step 2. Calculation of component cost of capital:

1. Component cost of debt:

Up to $4.0 million: k_d = .08 × (1 – .50) = .040
$4.01 million to $12 million: k_d = .09 × (1 – .50) = .045
Over $12 million: k_d = .10 × (1 – .50) = .050

2. Component cost of preferred:

Up to $2.0 million:	k_p = .090
$2.01 million to $6 million:	k_p = .100
Over $6 million:	k_p = .110

3. Component cost of common stock:

$$\frac{\text{EPS (1971)}}{\text{EPS (1964)}} = \frac{\$2.60}{\$1.52} = 1.711$$

In the table of compound sums (Appendix table A-1), the factor 1.711 (approximately) appears in the row for seven years in the 8 percent column—this implies an 8 percent growth rate:

Stockholders' approximate required rate of return

$$k = \frac{D}{P} + g = \frac{\$2.60}{\$65.00} + 0.08 = 0.04 + 0.08 = \underline{0.12} = \underline{12\%}$$

Up to $8 million new outside equity

$$k_e = \frac{.12}{1 - \dfrac{\$5}{\$65}} = .1300 = 13.00\%$$

Over $8 million new outside equity

$$k_e = \frac{.12}{1 - \dfrac{\$10}{\$65}} = .1418 = 14.18\%$$

Step 3. Calculations of average and marginal cost of capital at various asset expansion levels: See the table on page 117.

$10,000,000

	$ Amt.	Weight	×	Cost	=	Product
Debt	$ 4.0	.400	×	.040	=	0.01600
Preferred	2.0	.200	×	.090	=	0.01800
Equity	4.0					
Retained earnings	$ 4.0	.400	×	.120	=	0.04800
New common stock	–0–					
Average cost of new capital						0.08200
						8.200%

$30,000,000

	$ Amt.	Weight	×	Cost	=	Product
Debt	$12.0	.400	×	.045	=	0.01800
Preferred	$ 6.0	.200	×	.100	=	0.02000
Equity	12.0					
Retained earnings	$ 4.0	.133	×	.120	=	0.01596
New common stock	8.0	.266	×	.130	=	0.03458
Average cost of new capital						0.08854
						8.854%

$50,000,000

	$ Amt.	Weight	×	Cost	=	Product
Debt	$20.0	.400	×	.0500	=	0.02000
Preferred	10.0	.200	×	.1100	=	0.02200
Equity	20.0					
Retained earnings	$ 4.0	.080	×	.1200	=	0.00960
New common stock	16.0	.320	×	.1418	=	0.04538
Average cost of new capital						0.09698
						9.698%

$10,000,000

	Weight	×	Marginal cost	=	Product
Debt	.40	×	.0400	=	0.01600
Preferred	.20	×	.0900	=	0.01800
Equity	.40	×	.1200	=	0.04800
Marginal cost of new capital					0.08200
					8.200%

$30,000,000

	Weight	×	Marginal cost	=	Product
Debt	.40	×	.0450	=	0.01800
Preferred	.20	×	.1000	=	0.02000
Equity	.40	×	.1300	=	0.05200
Marginal cost of new capital					0.09000
					9.000%

$50,000,000

	Weight	×	Marginal cost	=	Product
Debt	.40	×	.0500	=	0.02000
Preferred	.20	×	.1100	=	0.02200
Equity	.40	×	.1418	=	0.05672
Marginal cost of new capital					0.09872
					9.872%

b. Graph of average and marginal cost of capital

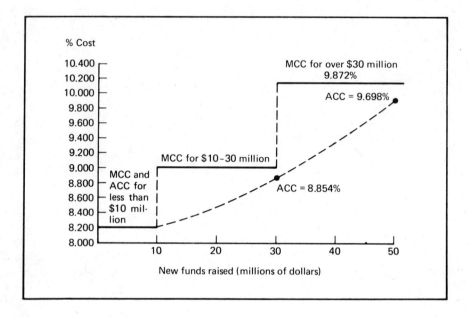

Chapter 13

Dividend Policy and Internal Financing

Theme: Dividend policy affects the financial structure, the flow of funds, corporate liquidity, and investor attitudes. Thus, it is one of the central financial decision areas related to policies seeking to maximize the value of the firm's common stock.

I. These are legal rules influencing dividend policy.
  A. The *net profits rule* states that dividends must be paid from past and present earnings.
  B. The *capital impairment rule* states that dividends cannot be paid out of invested capital.
  C. The *insolvency rule* states that no dividends can be paid during insolvency.

II. Business factors affecting dividend policy include:
  A. A *high rate of profit* on net worth makes it desirable to retain earnings rather than to pay them out if the investor will earn less on them.
  B. A *high rate of asset expansion* creates a need to retain funds rather than to pay dividends.
  C. *Stability of earnings* will allow a high payout ratio which can be maintained even during difficult economic times.
  D. *Age and size of firm* influences the ease of access to capital markets.
  E. The cash or *liquidity position* of a firm influences its ability to pay dividends.
  F. Its *need to repay debt* also influences the availability of cash flow to pay dividends.
  G. *Control considerations* may influence dividend policy, since additional external financing is influenced by the dividend payout.
  H. Maintenance of a *target dividend* will lead to low payouts when profits are temporarily high and to high payouts when profits are temporarily depressed. This will cause dividend growth to lag profit growth.
  I. The *tax position of stockholders* also affects dividend policy. Corporations owned largely by taxpayers in high income tax brackets tend toward lower dividend payouts. Corporations owned by small investors tend toward higher dividend payouts. However, if a firm's growth possibilities suggest a low pay-

out, there will be a tendency for it to attract stockholders who do not want current dividends.

J. In addition, the *tax position of the corporation* affects its dividend policies. Possible penalties for excess accumulation of retained earnings may cause dividend payouts to be higher than financial considerations alone would indicate.

III. Theory of dividend policy.

A. A basic principle is a comparison of the rate at which the corporation can earn on reinvested retained earnings compared with the best rate a stockholder could earn if he received earnings in the form of dividends.

1. The personal income tax rates on dividends must be taken into account.

2. Retained earnings avoid flotation costs as compared with raising equity funds externally.

B. A very important consideration is the investment opportunities available to the firm.

1. An investment opportunity schedule, or internal rate of return schedule, may be drawn.

2. The amount of retained earnings available affects the shape of the firm's marginal cost of capital.

C. Generally, as in economic theory, the maximizing decision reflects the intersection of the relevant demand and supply functions.

1. The internal rate of return schedules are related to the firm's cost of capital functions.

2. Alternative opportunities of the firm need to be considered.

a. Repurchase of its stock.

b. Acquisition of other corporations with high internal rates of return.

D. The above framework can be reconciled to the concept of a target dividend payout ratio.

IV. There is a theoretical dispute regarding dividend policy. The dispute centers upon the psychology of the investor in relation to the choice of whether earnings should be taken as capital gains or as dividend payments. Dividends are probably less risky than capital gains. However, dividends are taxed at a higher rate than capital gains.

A. Gordon, Lintner, and others have suggested that cash flows from a firm with a low payout ratio will be capitalized at higher rates than those of a high payout firm, because investors think that capital gains resulting from earnings retention are more risky than are dividend payments.

B. The approach typified by Miller and Modigliani holds that a change in dividends affects the price of a firm's stock primarily because it provides information about expected future earnings. Miller and Modigliani believe that investors, on balance, are indifferent between returns coming in the form of dividends or capital gains.

C. A third approach, favored by the authors of this text, is that neither set of generalizations hold. Rather, the optimum dividend policy varies from firm to firm depending upon the following:

1. The tax status and current income needs of the stockholders.
2. The firm's internal investment opportunities.
3. Other conditions of the firm in question, including its long-run plans and objectives.

V. Patterns in dividend payouts.

  A. Dividends are more stable than earnings.

    1. Studies have indicated a tendency toward a stable dollar dividend.

    2. Advantages of a stable dividend policy include these:

      a. The more certain the dividends are, the lower the capitalization rate and, therefore, the higher the market price of the stock.

      b. Stockholders who live on income received in the form of dividends seek a relatively assured minimum dollar dividend.

      c. If stable dividends cause a lower payout ratio and if the firm's rate of return is greater than the market rate, a higher market price should result.

      d. Qualification for legal lists (that is, listing of securities in which institutions of a fiduciary nature are allowed to invest) requires a stable and uninterrupted dividend history. Placement on legal lists increases the breadth of the market and the potential demand for the firm's securities.

  B. Between 1870 and 1939 NYSE corporations paid out approximately two-thirds of earnings in the form of dividends.

  C. The dividend payout rate has varied.

    1. In the early post-war period it dropped below 40 percent.

    2. During the decade of the fifties it rose to 45 percent.

    3. In the early sixties it rose to 50 percent while investment opportunities were still limited.

    4. With an increase in the growth rate in the economy and increased investment opportunities, as well as tight money, payout ratios dropped again in the late 1960s.

VI. Dividend payout patterns among industries.

  A. Low dividend payout patterns have been used by firms in industries with favorable investment opportunities and rapid growth rates.

    1. Electronics.

    2. Office equipment.

    3. Color television.

  B. Slow growth industries have had higher dividend payouts.

    1. Cigarette manufacturing.

    2. Textiles.

    3. Coal mining.

  C. Industries growing at about the same rate as the general economy have an average dividend payout.

    1. Oil.

    2. Steel.

    3. Banking.

  D. The above patterns fit into the theory of dividend payouts which relates the firm's investment opportunities to its cost of capital.

VII. Dividend payments.

  A. Management generally tries to convey to investors certain ideas:

    1. The regular dividend will be maintained.

    2. Earnings will be sufficient to maintain dividends.

  B. In order to attain these goals, what may firms with volatile cash flows and investment needs do?

    1. They will set a lower regular dividend rate than firms with the same average earnings but less volatility.

    2. They may also declare extra dividends in years when earnings are high and funds are available.

VIII. The payment procedure is as follows:

  A. Directors declare the dividend and the payment date.

  B. On the *holder of record* date the stock transfer books are closed.

  C. The right to the dividend expires on the *ex-dividend* date.

  D. The company mails checks to the holders of record on the payment date.

IX. Stock dividends and stock splits are discussed.

  A. There are some distinctions between them.

    1. A stock dividend is a transfer of earned surplus to the capital stock account and a concomitant pro-rata distribution of stock to the owners.

    2. A stock split simply increases the number of shares outstanding.

  B. There are also some similarities.

    1. No cash is distributed in either case.

    2. Both result in a larger number of shares outstanding.

    3. Total net worth remains unchanged.

    4. In a practical sense, there is no difference between the two. The NYSE recognizes this by defining a stock dividend as a stock distribution up to 24 percent of the outstanding stock of the firm, and a stock split as any distribution of 25 percent or more.

  C. Identifying characteristics.

    1. A split does not affect the capital accounts, whereas a stock dividend increases the capital stock account and reduces earned surplus.

    2. A split may result in change of the par or stated value, but a stock dividend does not.

  D. Among the effects of splits or dividends are these:

    1. Effect on the market price of the stock depends on prospective changes in underlying earning power reflected in current or announced changes in dividend payouts.

    2. Cash conservation is accomplished to a degree. However, the total amounts paid out for dividends will increase if the effective dividend rate is increased for the larger number of shares.

3. Tax benefit accrues to stockholders in payment of capital gains tax rather than income taxes on cash dividends.

4. Number of shareholders is increased by reducing the unit price of stock to a more popular trading range.

PROBLEMS

13-1. A firm plans a $30 million expansion in net assets during the coming year. Given a debt-assets ratio of 40 percent (considered to be optimal), earnings after taxes of $60 million, and a dividend payout policy of 80 percent, how much external equity must the firm seek?

Solution:

$60,000,000, earnings
×   0.8, payout rate
$48,000,000, dividends

$60,000,000, earnings
−48,000,000, dividends
$12,000,000, retained earnings

$30,000,000, capital budget (net assets added)
        ×0.6, 1.0−(debt-assets ratio), or % of total to be financed with
                  equity 1.0 − 0.4 = 0.6
$18,000,000, new equity needed

$18,000,000, new equity needed
−12,000,000, retained earnings
$ 6,000,000, external equity needed

13-2. An increase in which of the following is likely to *decrease* a firm's ability or willingness to pay dividends?
a. Current ratio.
b. Target growth rate in assets.
c. Debt ratio.
d. Rate of return on assets.
e. b and c.
f. c and d.

Solution: e.

13-3. A decrease in which of the following is likely to *decrease* a firm's willingness to pay dividends?
a. Earnings stability.
b. Access to capital market.
c. Investment opportunities.
d. Net worth/total assets ratio.

e. a, c, and d.
f. a, b, and d.
g. c, and d.

Solution:

f.

13-4. What does the residual theory of dividend policy assert?

Solution: Dividends are paid out of the residual remaining after internal investments by the firm.

13-5. On February 1, the directors of Westbrig Corporation met and declared the regular quarterly dividend of $2.50 per share to holders of record on March 15, payment to be made April 1. You own 400 shares of Westbrig stock, 100 shares purchased on each of the following dates: February 15, March 1, March 10, and March 15. What total dividends will you receive? (The stock goes ex-dividends four days prior to the date of record.)

Solution:

February 15:	100 shares
March 1:	100 shares
March 10:	100 shares
	300

$ 2.50, dividend per share
X 300, shares
$750.00, total dividends received

13-6. ABC Corporation has retained earnings of $600,000, capital stock of $300,000, and capital surplus of $80,000. Its common stock is selling for $50 per share. 100,000 shares are currently outstanding. If the firm now declares and distributes a 5 percent stock dividend, what balances will the capital stock, capital surplus, and retained earnings accounts show?

Solution:

Step 1: $\dfrac{\$300,000 \text{ capital stock}}{100,000 \text{ shares outstanding}}$ = $3.00, par value.

Therefore the amount that will be added to the capital stock account is (5,000 × $3.00 par value) = <u>$15,000.</u>

Step 2: 100,000, shares outstanding
        <u>×   5%, % stock dividend</u>
             5,000, shares issued in stock dividend

        5,000, shares × $50 market value = $250,000

transferred from retained earnings, with $15,000 to capital stock and $235,000 to capital surplus.

Step 3: Capital stock ($300,000 + $15,000) = <u>$315,000</u>

        Capital surplus ($80,000 + $235,000) = <u>$315,000</u>

        Retained earnings ($600,000 − $250,000) = <u>$350,000.</u>

13-7. What is the effect of a stock dividend on book value per share?

Solution: It will tend to decrease book value per share.

13-8. The market price of XYZ's stock was $45 per share prior to splitting 3-for-1 last month. The firm's $2.00 dividend on the new (split) shares is an increase of 5 percent over the previous dividend on the presplit stock. What was the presplit dividend per share?

Solution:

$2.00, postsplit dividend
<u>×   3</u>
$6.00, equivalent presplit dividend

$6.00 = 1.05X

  X = $5.71, previous presplit dividend

Part V

Working Capital Management

Chapter 14
Current Asset Management

Theme: Current asset management, or working capital management, involves a large portion of the firm's total assets, as more than half the typical firm's total investment is in current assets. This chapter focuses on principles and techniques used for effective control of investment in current assets. Principles for controlling investment in cash, marketable securities, accounts receivable, and inventories are developed, and the general application of these principles is discussed.

I. Current asset management is important for these reasons:
  A. A great deal of the financial manager's time is allocated to working capital management and the day-to-day operations of the firm.
  B. More than half of the total assets are typically invested in current assets.
  C. Growth of sales results in increased investment in current assets.
  D. Investment in fixed assets may be reduced by renting or leasing, but investment in inventories and receivables is unavoidable.
II. Controlling investment in cash and marketable securities.
  A. There are three primary reasons for holding cash:
    1. Transactions motive.
    2. Precautionary motive.
    3. Speculative motive.
  B. Adequate cash provides certain benefits.
    1. Sufficient cash permits taking trade discounts.
    2. Adequate cash is required to strengthen the current and acid test ratios, which are key items in the appraisal of the firm's credit position.
    3. Ample cash is desirable to take advantage of favorable business opportunities.
    4. Adequate cash is necessary to provide the firm with sufficient liquidity to meet various emergencies.
  C. The strength of the precautionary motive depends upon two things:
    1. The predictability of cash inflows and outflows.
    2. The firm's ability to borrow on short notice.
  D. Large accumulations of cash for speculative purposes are rarely found.

E. Usually, both the precautionary and speculative motives are largely satisfied by holdings of marketable securities, which may be regarded as "near money" assets.

F. Methods of improving the inflow-outflow pattern of cash and thereby conserving cash include:

1. Synchronization of cash flows:
    a. Frequent requisitioning of funds by division offices from the central office.
    b. Effective forecasting to reduce the cash on hand to meet actual requirements.
2. Reduction of float:
    a. Float refers to funds in transit between cities.
    b. The lock-box plan provides for a post office collection box in a customer's city where pickups are made by a bank in that city. The checks are cleared in the local area and the collecting bank remits by wire to the seller's bank of deposit.

III. Investment of funds.

A. A firm may have cash to invest for the following reasons:

1. Seasonal or cyclical fluctuations.
2. Accumulation of resources as protection against a number of contingencies.

B. Alternative marketable securities for investments:

1. U.S. Treasury bills.
2. U.S. Treasury certificates.
3. U.S. Treasury notes.
4. Prime commercial paper.
5. Negotiable certificates of deposit.
6. Savings certificates at commercial banks.
7. Savings accounts at commercial·banks.
8. Savings accounts at savings and loan associations.
9. Bonds and stocks of other corporations.
10. Bonds and stocks of the firm in question.

C. These considerations affect the choice of securities:

1. Maturity, yields, and risks must be appropriate to the firm's needs.
2. Investment in firms in related fields may be desirable because:
    a. The nature and future of these firms is familiar.
    b. The investments may provide easy access to market information.
3. However, antitrust considerations may preclude this option for larger firms.

IV. Management of investment in receivables is explained.

A. Typical ratios are as follows:

1. For manufacturing firms a ratio of receivables to sales of 8–12 percent.
2. An average collection period of one month.
3. A ratio of receivables to total assets centering around 16–20 percent.

B. The major determinants of the level of receivables include:
1. Volume of credit sales.
2. Seasonality of sales.
3. Rules for credit limits.
4. Terms of sale and credit policies of individual firms.
5. Collection policies.
C. Determinants of credit policy include the following:
1. The industry's characteristic credit terms.
2. The evaluation of credit risk—the Cs of credit.
   a. Character—The probability that the customer will try to honor his obligation.
   b. Capacity—Subjective judgment or evaluation of the ability of the customer to pay.
   c. Capital—Measured by the general financial position of the firm as indicated by financial ratio analysis.
   d. Collateral—Represented by assets the customer may offer as a pledge for security.
   e. Conditions—The impact of general economic trends on the firm or special developments in certain areas of the economy.
D. Sources of credit information.
1. Previous experience with the customer.
2. Work of the local credit associations, including:
   a. Credit interchange through the National Association of Credit management.
   b. Periodic meetings of local industry groups.
3. Credit reporting agencies, such as these:
   a. Dun & Bradstreet.
      1. Widest coverage.
      2. A reference book, published six times a year, with credit ratings of firms.
   b. Agencies specializing in coverage of a limited number of industries.
      1. National Credit Office.
      2. Lyon Furniture Mercantile Agency.
E. Use of credit ratings in credit decisions is discussed.
1. Two types of information are provided:
   a. Financial strength.
   b. Composite credit appraisal.
2. Credit reports provide more detailed information:
   a. History of customer.
   b. Discussion of business operations and location.
   c. Financial information.
   d. Payment experience.
3. Risk class groupings can be developed on basis of above information indi-

cating probable loss ratio as a percentage of total sales to firms in that risk group.

4. The probable loss ratio may be related to the firm's margin of profit and overhead in relation to revenues.

5. Credit limits set a maximum on the total amount of credit without a detailed review of the customer.

   a. It may be related to experience with the customer.

   b. If there has been no experience, it may be related to probable loss ratio.

   c. It may be a fraction of the firm's net worth.

V. The management of investment in inventories must include:

A. General levels of inventories.

   1. Inventory-to-sales ratios are generally concentrated in the 12–20 percent range.

   2. Inventory-to-total assets ratios usually range from 16–30 percent.

B. General determinants of investment in inventory are:

   1. Level of sales.

   2. Length and technical nature of the production processes.

   3. Durability versus perishability or style factor in the end product.

C. Types of inventories are the following:

   1. Raw materials.

   2. Work in process.

   3. Finished goods.

D. Determinants of the levels of raw materials inventories include:

   1. Anticipated production.

   2. Seasonality of production.

   3. Reliability of supply sources.

   4. Efficiency of scheduling purchases.

   5. Production operations.

E. Determinants of work in process inventories:

   1. Length of the production period.

   2. Make versus buy decisions.

F. Determinants of the level of finished goods inventories:

   1. Coordination of production and sales.

   2. Influenced by credit terms and credit policies.

G. Inventory decision models—economical order quantity—are discussed below:

   1. A method of controlling investment in inventory.

   2. Formula:

$$EOQ = \sqrt{\frac{2 \times F \times S}{C}} = \sqrt{\frac{2 \times 10 \times 100}{1 \times 0.2}} = 100 \text{ units}$$

where EOQ = economical order quantity

$\quad$ S $\quad$ = sales for the period in units = 100

$\quad$ C $\quad$ = carrying cost per unit of inventory

$\quad$ F $\quad$ = fixed cost per order = \$10

$\quad$ A $\quad$ = average inventory = $\dfrac{EOQ}{2}$ = 50 units + safety stock

$\quad$ a. The larger the sales per period or processing costs per order, the larger the EOQ.

$\quad$ b. The larger the inventory carrying charge, the smaller the EOQ.

$\quad$ 3. Two contributions of EOQ control methods are these:

$\quad$ a. They help achieve sound inventory management.

$\quad$ b. They provide a basis for projecting requirements for investment in inventories.

H. Inventory analysis is generalized.

$\quad$ 1. Managing all types of assets is basically an inventory-type problem.

$\quad$ a. A basic stock to balance inflows and outflows is necessary.

$\quad$ b. Safety stocks for the unexpected are needed.

$\quad$ c. Anticipation stocks for future growth needs should be considered.

$\quad$ 2. Size of investment results in rising and falling costs.

$\quad$ a. Costs that rise with larger inventories are these:

$\quad\quad$ 1. Warehousing.

$\quad\quad$ 2. Interest on funds tied up in inventories.

$\quad\quad$ 3. Insurance.

$\quad\quad$ 4. Obsolescence.

$\quad$ b. Costs that fall with size of inventories are these:

$\quad\quad$ 1. Fewer production interruptions.

$\quad\quad$ 2. Fewer losses of sales because of inventory shortages.

$\quad\quad$ 3. Greater variety of styles and size.

$\quad$ 3. Decision rule: choose that inventory investment where the curves for the two types of cost intersect; this will minimize the combined inventory investment costs.

VI. Cash management may be considered as an inventory problem.

A. Optimum cash balances can be found by the use of inventory type models.

B. Cash inflows are represented by the "orders" of an inventory model. These come from the following:

$\quad$ 1. Receipts.

$\quad$ 2. Borrowing.

$\quad$ 3. Sale of securities.

C. Primary "carrying costs" of cash are the opportunity costs of the lost interest payments.

D. The principal "ordering costs" are brokerage fees.

PROBLEMS

14-1. The JPC Corporation reports $2,500,000 in purchases of materials for the year. Outstanding accounts payable total $325,000. How many days' purchases remain outstanding?

Solution:

a. $\dfrac{\$325,000 \text{ accounts payable}}{\$2,500,000 \text{ purchases}} = 0.130$

b. $0.13 \times 360 \text{ days} = 46.8 \text{ days}$

14-2. If a firm sells on terms of net 60 days and its accounts are, on the average, 30 days overdue, what will its investment in receivables be? (Annual credit sales are $800,000.)

Solution:

60 net
30 overdue
90 days

$90/360 = \frac{1}{4} \times \$800,000 \text{ credit sales} = \$200,000$, accounts receivable

14-3. The Pettit Production Company has sales of $60 million a year in a good year and $40 million in a poor year. Its fixed assets are $25 million; receivables and inventories are 35 percent of sales; total assets are constant at $50 million. The firm must have liquidity because of substantial risks involved in the production of a new product. In addition, the firm must be ready to meet effective foreign competitors. How much cash does the firm have available for investment in good years? In poor years?

Solution:

	Good Year*	Bad Year*
Sales	$ 60	$ 40
Fixed assets	25	25
Receivables and inventories**	21	14
Total operating assets	$ 46	$ 39
Total assets	$ 50	$ 50
Total operating assets	−46	−39
Cash available for investment	$ 4	$ 11

The above results indicate that higher levels of sales utilize greater amounts of cash.

*Amounts in millions.
**.35 times sales.

14-4. A firm expects its annual sales rate to double within the next few months. Current sales are 50,000 units at a cost of $5 a unit. Order processing costs will remain at $20.00 an order, but inventory carrying charges are expected to increase from $.75 to $1.00 because of additional storage and handling requirements.

a. If the firm wishes to minimize inventory costs, what is the optimal number of orders it will utilize once the annual sales level is achieved?

b. At what inventory level should a reorder be made, if the desired safety stock is 300 units (on hand initially), and one week is required for delivery? Assume 50 weeks in a year.

Solution:

a. EOQ = economical order quantity
   S = sales for period in units
   P = price paid per unit
   F = purchasing cost per order
   C = inventory carrying charge

$$EOQ = \sqrt{\frac{2 \times S \times F}{C}}$$

$$EOQ = \sqrt{\frac{2 \times 100,000 \times 20.00}{\$1}} = \sqrt{\frac{4,000,000}{\$1}}$$

$$EOQ = 2,000 \text{ units}$$

$$\frac{sales}{EOQ} = \frac{100,000}{2,000} = 50 \text{ orders}$$

b. Weekly rate of use $= \dfrac{100,000 \text{ units}}{50 \text{ weeks in a year}} = 2,000 \text{ units}$

Reorder point $= 300 + 1\,(2,000) = 2,300$ units

Chapter 15
Major Sources of Short-Term Financing

Theme: Major sources of short-term financing are analyzed from the viewpoint of the financial manager.

I. Trade credit.
   A. Purchase of materials or supplies on credit from other firms is recorded as accounts payable.
   B. Trade credit is a "spontaneous" source of financing in that it arises from ordinary business transactions.
   C. Trade credit is the largest category of short-term financing, and is especially important for smaller firms which do not have access to other capital markets.
   D. Credit terms are determined by the following:
      1. Economic nature of the product:
         a. Turnover.
         b. Perishability.
      2. Seller circumstances:
         a. Financial strength of sellers.
         b. Size of seller.
         c. Use in sales promotion.
         d. Degree of excess capacity.
      3. Buyer circumstances:
         a. Degree of financial strength.
         b. Risks associated with the product.
   E. Cash discounts may be given.
      1. Savings from the discount frequently exceed the rate of interest on borrowed funds; therefore, trade credit can be expensive.
      2. The length of credit is influenced by the size of the discounts offered.
   F. Forms in which credit terms are expressed:
      1. Individual order terms: for example, 1/10, n/30; 2/10, n/60; and so on.
      2. Lumped-order terms and billing: End of Month (EOM); Middle of Month (MOM).

3. Dating: 7/10-60; 2/10-60; Receipt of Goods (ROG).

G. Implicit cost of trade credit.

  1. Price of the merchandise may be higher or its quality lower.

  2. May be measured directly if a cash discount is involved.

    a. Formula:

$$\text{cost} = \frac{\text{discount percent}}{(100 - \text{discount percent})}$$

$$\times \frac{360}{(\text{max. days credit} - \text{discount period})}$$

    b. Illustration—terms of 2/10, net 30.

$$\text{cost} = \frac{2}{100 - 2} \times \frac{360}{30 - 10} = 0.0204 \times 18 = 36.72\%$$

H. Advantages of trade credit as a source of financing.

  1. Convenient and informal.

  2. Wise use promotes sound customer relations.

  3. A firm that does not qualify for credit from a financial institution may receive credit from the seller because of the latter's acquaintance with the firm.

  4. Cost may be higher or lower.

    a. Cost commensurate with risks to the seller.

    b. Buyer may not have better alternatives.

    c. Sometimes the buyer has not calculated the cost of trade credit.

II. Commercial bank loans.

A. Importance.

  1. Banks occupy a pivotal position in the short-term money market.

  2. Banks often provide the marginal credit that allows firms to expand.

B. Characteristics.

  1. Forms of loans—single loan, credit line.

  2. Size of loans—mostly small in number, large in dollar amount.

  3. Maturity—concentration on the short-term lending market.

  4. Security—high-risk borrowers must provide collateral.

  5. Minimum average balance—usually 15–20 percent of loan is required as "compensating balance."

  6. Repayment of bank loans—"clean up" required for firms to demonstrate ability to repay.

C. Measuring the effective costs of bank loans.

  1. Interest rates are quoted in three ways.

    a. Regular compound interest.

    b. Discount interest.

c. Installment interest.
2. Compensating balances may increase effective cost.
3. Fees may also be charged.
D. In choosing a bank, the financial manager should consider:
1. The bank's policy toward risk.
2. The availability of management counseling services.
3. The loyalty of the bank when the firm encounters difficulties.
4. The stability of the bank's deposits as a measure of possible repayment pressure.
5. Coinciding of the loan areas in which the bank specializes with the borrower's area of operations.
6. The maximum size loan a bank can make.
7. The financial and business services offered by the bank.
III. Commercial paper.
A. Nature—Consists of promissory notes of large firms that are sold primarily to other business firms, insurance companies, investment funds, pension funds, and small banks.
B. Maturities vary from two to six months with an average of about five months.
C. Costs are generally about one-fourth to one-half of 1 percent below the prime rate.
D. Use—The use of open market for commercial paper is limited to firms which are good credit risks.
1. Advantages:
a. Use of commercial paper market effects the broadest and most advantageous use of capital markets.
b. It provides more funds at lower rates than do other methods, especially since compensating balances are not required.
c. Borrower avoids the inconvenience and expense of financing arrangements.
d. Publicity and prestige are enhanced.
e. Some counseling from the commercial paper dealer is available.
2. Disadvantages:
a. Amount of funds available limited to the excess liquidity of the main suppliers of funds at a particular time.
b. A commercial paper borrower who is in temporary financial difficulty receives little consideration because of the impersonal nature of commercial paper market.
3. Use has increased greatly during the tight money period since mid-1966.
a. From the borrower's standpoint, the availability of bank credit has been reduced.
b. From the viewpoint of lenders, yields are often higher than on other low-risk short-term investments.

IV. Use of security in short-term financing.
   A. Security may be offered:
     1. If the borrower's credit is not sufficient to justify a loan.
     2. If lenders will quote lower interest rates for a secured loan.
   B. Types of collateral offered:
     1. Marketable stocks or bonds—few firms hold these.
     2. Real property and equipment—usually used to secure long-term loans.
     3. Short-term assets—most frequently offered.
       a. Accounts receivable.
       b. Inventories.
V. Accounts receivable financing.
   A. Two major forms.
     1. In *pledging* no notification is made to the buyer of the goods, and the lender has recourse to the holder of the accounts receivable in case of default. The receivable is *not* sold to the lender; it is merely used to secure a loan.
     2. In *factoring* the buyer of the goods makes payment directly to the factor, and the factor has no recourse to the seller of the goods in case of default. The receivable *is* sold outright to the lender.
   B. Procedure for pledging accounts receivable.
     1. A contract setting forth legal rights and procedures is agreed upon.
     2. The firm takes its invoices to the financial institution, where they are reviewed and either accepted or rejected.
     3. Upon acceptance, payment is made to the firm.
     4. When the buyer of the goods makes payment to the firm, the proceeds are turned over to the financial institution.
     5. Normally, the firms which use this service are small, and about half of the individual invoices are under $250.
   C. Procedure for factoring accounts receivable.
     1. A legal contract is drawn up.
     2. The firm receives an order for goods.
     3. The purchase order is drawn up and sent to the factor for a credit check.
     4. If the factor disapproves the purchase order, the selling firm can make the sale but the seller bears the credit risk.
     5. If the factor approves the purchase order, it is processed and the invoice is stamped with instructions to remit payment to the factor.
     6. For a small firm the credit checking service of the factor can be utilized as a cost-saving device.
   D. The cost of receivable financing.
     1. Accounts receivable pledging rates normally range from 8 to 12 percent a year.
     2. Factoring charges are composed of two elements:
       a. A fee for credit checking ranging from ½–2 percent.

b. An interest charge of 8–12 percent. The interest charge is prorated over the period for which the funds are outstanding; that is, it is an annual rate.

E. Advantages of receivable financing.

1. It is a flexible method.
2. The security provided may make financing possible.
3. Factoring may provide the services of a credit department.

F. Disadvantages of accounts receivable financing.

1. When invoices are numerous, administrative costs may be high.
2. The firm is using a highly liquid asset as security.

G. Evaluation and future use.

1. The method has contributed to the financing of smaller firms and marginal credit risks.
2. Automation will reduce the costs and increase the convenience of employing receivables financing. Credit card use is a prime example of a type of automated accounts receivable financing.

VI. Inventory financing.

A. Major forms.

1. Blanket security agreement.
2. Trust receipts.
3. Field warehousing.

B. Chattel mortgage.

1. Is a lien against other than real property.
2. Disadvantageous to lender in that inventory can be sold.

C. Trust receipts.

1. Definition—an instrument acknowledging that the borrower holds goods in trust for the lender.
2. Disadvantages.
   a. Must be issued for specific goods.
   b. Other complex legal requirements.
3. The borrower may keep the goods in his possession, but must remit the proceeds of the sale of the specific goods to the lender.

D. Field warehousing.

1. Establishment requires two elements.
   a. Public notification of the arrangement.
   b. Providing supervision over the warehouse.
2. Financing procedure.
   a. Goods are delivered to the field warehouse.
   b. Custodian describes the goods and notifies the lender of the delivery.
   c. Lender deposits funds for the use of the borrower.
   d. Borrower receives purchase orders and transmits them to the lender.
   e. Lender notifies the custodian to release the goods.

PROBLEMS

15-1. How much additional trade credit will be spontaneously generated if a firm which previously averaged $1,500 of purchases a day (on terms of net 20) now doubles its purchases and simultaneously gets new credit terms of net 30?

Solution:

$3,000 purchases × 30 days = $90,000, payables
$1,500 purchases × 20 days = <u>30,000,</u> payables
$60,000, additional trade credit

15-2. If a firm is unable to take advantage of available cash discounts at all times, which credit terms should it find least desirable, all other things constant?
a. 1/10 net 20.   d. 2/10 net 30.
b. 2/10 net 20.   e. Indifferent between *a* and *c*.
c. 1/10 net 30.

Solution: a. 1/10 net 20 offers the smallest discount and the shortest terms.

15-3. Given credit terms of 1/10 net 20, what is the cost, on an annual basis, of not taking the cash discount?

Solution: Use the following formula:

$$\text{Cost} = \frac{\text{discount percent}}{(100 - \text{discount}\%)} \times \frac{360 \text{ days}}{(\text{final due date} - \text{discount period})}$$

$$= \frac{1}{99} \times \frac{360}{10} = 36.36\%$$

15-4. A firm needs $90,000 to pay off outstanding obligations. A local bank will make the loan but requires a 15 percent compensating balance. (The company would ordinarily keep a zero balance.) If the stated rate of interest is 6 percent, what is the effective cost?

Solution:

$$\frac{0.06 \text{ nominal cost}}{0.85\% \text{ of funds received}} = 7.06\%, \text{ effective rate } or$$

a. $0.85\ X\ =\ \$\ 90{,}000$ net loan

$X\ =\ \$105{,}882$ gross loan

b. $\$105{,}882.00$

$\times\quad\ 0.06$

$\overline{\$\quad 6{,}352.92}$ interest cost

c. $\dfrac{\$6{,}352.92\ \text{interest cost}}{\$90{,}000\ \text{funds received}} = 7.06\%$, effective rate

15-5. A firm borrows on a 1-year bank note at 7 percent effective rate of interest. The total interest payment, $400, is deducted from the loan amount at the time the loan is issued. If the firm repays the loan in 12 equal monthly installments, what is the amount of the note? (Interest tables are not necessary for this problem.)

Solution:

$$\$400\ =\ \text{interest payment}$$
$$X\ =\ \text{gross loan}$$
$$(X\ -\ \$400)\ =\ \text{net loan}$$
$$(X\ -\ \$400)/2\ =\ \text{average funds available over the year}$$

$$\frac{\$400\ \text{interest cost}}{(X\ -\ \$400)/2\ \text{average funds received}} = 0.07,\ \text{effective rate of interest}$$

$$\$800\ =\ 0.07(X\ -\ \$400)$$
$$X\ =\ \$11{,}829$$

15-6. A large manufacturing firm has been selling on 1/10 net 30 basis. If the firm changes its credit terms to 2/10 net 20, what change might be anticipated on the balance sheet of its customers?

Solution: Other things constant, the higher cash discount will give customers more incentive to make payment early and payables will decrease. Also, the shorter credit terms will cause an increase in bank loans for the purpose of meeting payments.

15-7. A large firm has just sold an issue of six-month commercial paper. The paper carries an interest rate of 4 percent. Which of the choices below is most likely to be the current prime rate?

a. Above 5½ percent.   d. 4 percent.

b. 5 percent.   e. Below 4 percent.

c. 4½ percent.

Solution: c. Commercial paper issued by large, reputable firms typically carries an interest rate slightly below the prime rate. Therefore, 4½ percent is the most likely value for the prime rate.

15-8. A firm has just negotiated a $25,000 loan with its bank. The stated rate of interest is 6 percent. If the bank discounts the loan, what is the effective rate of interest? (The loan is repaid at the end of the year.)

Solution:

$$\frac{X\ \text{interest}}{\$25,000,\ \text{gross loan}} = 0.06,\ \text{stated interest rate}$$

$X = \$1,500,$ interest

$25,000,$ gross loan

$\underline{-1,500,}$ interest

$23,500,$ net loan

$$\frac{\$\ 1,500,\ \text{interest}}{\$23,500,\ \text{net loan}} = 6.38\%,\ \text{effective rate of interest}$$

15-9. In problem 15-8, what is the approximate effective rate of interest if interest is computed on the initial balance, the loan is not discounted, and the loan is paid back in 12-month equal installments?

Solution:

$$\frac{\$\ 1,500}{\$25,000} = 0.06$$

$$\frac{\$25,000}{2} = \$12,500,\ \text{average funds outstanding}$$

$$\frac{\$1,500}{\$12,500} = 12\%,\ \text{effective rate of interest}$$

15-10.

Kaplan Corporation—Balance sheet
as of December 31, 1972

Cash	$ 40,000	Accounts payable	$ 90,000
Marketable securities	60,000	Bank loans (5%)	65,000
Accounts receivable	75,000	Notes payable	50,000
Inventories	100,000	Current maturity of long-	
Other current assets	25,000	term debt	20,000
Total current assets	$300,000	Total current liabilities	$225,000
		Long-term debt	75,000
Fixed assets (net)	300,000	Net worth	300,000
Total assets	$600,000	Total liabilities	$600,000

Sales for the year: $1,200,000

a. If the sales/total assets ratio remains at 2 times, how much new financing will Kaplan need if sales rise by 12 percent?

Solution:

$1,200,000
  × 1.12
─────────
$1,344,000, new sales level

$$\frac{\$1,344,000}{X} = 2$$

X = $672,000, new assets level

  $672,000, new total assets level
− 600,000, total assets 1972
─────────
 $ 72,000, new asset financing needed

b. Kaplan's suppliers sell on credit terms of 30 days. Kaplan's payables presently represent 45 days of purchases. Other things remaining the same, what will Kaplan's debt ratio be after new short-term financing is used to bring the firm current on its trade obligations?

Solution: No change. The new short-term financing will equal the overdue payables, thus leaving the debt ratio unchanged.

c. In *b*, what will Kaplan's current ratio be if marketable securities are sold off to generate the funds necessary to become current on trade obligations?

Solution:

1. $$\frac{45 - 30}{45} = \frac{15}{45} = \frac{1}{3}$$

$\frac{1}{3}$ × $90,000, accounts payable (1972) = $30,000 marketable securities to be sold

2. $300,000, total current assets
  − 30,000, marketable securities to be sold
─────────
 $270,000, new current assets

3. $225,000, present current liabilities
  − 30,000, excess payables
─────────
 $195,000, new current liabilities

4. $\dfrac{\$270,000}{\$195,000} = 1.38$, current ratio

15-11. The Tompson Products Company has been growing rapidly. It is suffering from insufficient working capital, however, and has therefore become slow in paying bills. Of its total accounts payable, $200,000 is overdue. This threatens its relationship with its main supplier of equipment used in the manufacture of various kinds of battleships for the U.S. Navy. Over 90 percent of its sales are to four large defense contractors. Its balance sheet, sales and net profit for the year ended December 31, 1972, are shown here.

Tompson Products–Balance sheet,
December 31, 1972

Cash	$ 40,000	Trade credit*	$ 400,000
Receivables	600,000	Bank loans	280,000
Inventories		Accruals*	90,000
Raw material	50,000		
Work in process	300,000	Total current debt	770,000
Finished goods	80,000	Chattel mortgages	390,000
		Capital stock	140,000
Total current assets	1,070,000	Surplus	130,000
Equipment	360,000		
Total assets	$1,430,000	Total claims	$1,430,000
Sales	$2,500,000		
Profit after tax	130,000		

*Increases spontaneously with sales increases.

    a. If the same ratio of sales to total assets continues and if sales increase to $3,000,000, how much nonspontaneous financing, including retained earnings, will be required?

    b. Assume the facts listed below:

Receivables turn over five times a year (sales/receivables = 5)
All sales are made on credit
The factor requires a 9 percent reserve for returns and disputed items
The factor also requires a 3 percent commission to cover the costs of credit checking.
There is a 7 percent annual interest charge based on receivables less any reserve requirements and commissions. This payment is made at the beginning of the period and is deducted from the advance.

      1. What is the total amount of receivables outstanding at any time, when sales are $2.5 million?

2. How much cash does the firm actually receive by factoring the average amount of receivables?
3. What is the average duration of advances, on the basis of 360 days a year?
4. What is the total annual dollar cost of the financing?
5. What is the effective annual financing charge (percentage) paid on the money received?

Solution:

a. $\left[\dfrac{\text{assets}}{\text{sales}} - \dfrac{\text{spontaneous sources}}{\text{sales}} \right] \times \text{ increase in sales}$

$= \left[0.572 - 0.196 \times \$50,000 \right] = \$188,000 = \text{financing required}$

Note, however, that this figure is calculated on the assumption that accounts payable will continue overdue.

b. 1. Average receivables outstanding = ($2,500,000)/5 times = $500,000
   2. Cash actually received by firm:

> $500,000, average receivables, outstanding
> −45,000, reserve (9% of $500,000)
> $455,000
> −15,000, commission (3% of $500,000)
> $440,000, amount of advance after commission
> − 6,160, interest charge at 7% (see below)
> $433,840, cash actually received

Computation of interest charge:
Since the turnover rate of five times represents one-fifth of a year, or 72 days, the interest rate is one-fifth of 7 percent, or 1.4 percent. Applied to the base of $440,000 this rate is equal to $6,160.

3. Average duration of the advance is the collection period for the receivables, or 360 days/5, which equals 72 days.
4. Total cost of financing is the sum of the commission and interest costs: ($15,000 + $6,160) = $21,160
5. Effective annual financing charge $= \left[\dfrac{\$\ 21,160}{\$433,840} \right] \times 5 = 24.4\%$

Chapter 16

Intermediate-Term Financing

Theme: Intermediate-term financing is defined as liabilities originally scheduled for repayment in more than one but less than five years. It has been playing an increasingly important role because of its flexibility. The three major forms of intermediate-term financing include term loans, conditional sales contracts, and lease financing.

I. Term loans.

  A. A term loan is a business loan with a maturity of more than one year.

  B. Because term loans represent long-term fixed commitments, restrictive provisions are generally attached to them for the protection of the lender.

   1. The borrower must maintain a specified current ratio, and a specified minimum net working capital.

   2. Purchase of fixed assets is limited.

   3. Additional borrowing and future assumption of contingent liabilities are limited.

   4. An effort is made to insure the continuity of management.

   5. Financial statements and budgets are forwarded to the lender.

  C. The costs of term loans vary with the size of the loan and the strength of the borrowing firm.

   1. On loans of less than $500 the interest rate may be as high as 15 percent.

   2. On loans of $1 million and above, interest charges approximate the prime rate.

   3. Frequently, the interest charge is fixed as a function of the rediscount rate or the published prime rate of New York City banks; in this case, the cost of the loan could fluctuate.

  D. Other characteristics of term loans vary with the type of lender.

   1. Commercial bank term loans:

     a. Mature in from one to five years.

     b. Generally they are for amounts ranging from $100,000 to $250,000.

     c. Frequently they are made to companies with assets of less than $5 million.

      d. Frequently they are secured by stocks, bonds, machinery, or other equipment.

  2. Life insurance company and pension fund term loans:

      a. Mature in from five to fifteen years.

      b. Generally they are for amounts ranging from $1 million to $5 million.

      c. Generally they are made to large companies.

      d. Require collateral about one-third of the time, frequently in the form of real estate.

  3. Commercial banks and life insurance companies sometimes combine to make loans.

      a. Loans of over $10 million may be broken down into smaller amounts and financed in combination.

      b. A bank may make the loan for five years, with an insurance company taking it over for the segment with longer maturity.

E. Repayment provisions of term loans generally provide for amortization, or systematic repayment over the life of the loan.

  1. Repayment frequently is made possible from increased earnings due to the loan.

  2. The amortization schedule seeks to protect both the borrower and the lender.

  3. The amortization schedule is determined through the use of the formula:

$$R = \frac{A_n}{IF},$$

    where R = the amortization payment

        A_n = the amount of the loan

        IF = the appropriate interest factor (Table A-4).

  4. If loans are repaid ahead of schedule, a prepayment penalty equal to from 1-5 percent of the outstanding balance is usually required.

  5. A few term loans are not fully amortized and have a balloon segment at the end.

  6. In addition to fixed interest charges, institutional investors have increasingly taken additional compensation in the form of options to buy common shares. These options usually are in the form of detachable warrants permitting the purchase of the shares at stated prices over a designated period of time.

F. The major suppliers and users of term loans have changed over time.

  1. Industries with large investments in fixed assets tend to use term loans most frequently.

  2. A 1957 study showed that the greatest relative increase in the use of term loans was by industries characterized by small, rapidly growing firms.

3. In earlier periods, over half of all term loans were made to refund bonds sold at higher interest rates.

4. More recently, term loans have been used for working capital and to finance plant and equipment additions.

G. Evaluation of term loans:

  1. Advantages:

    a. Avoid possible nonrenewal of short-term loans.

    b. Avoid public flotation costs.

    c. Minimal negotiation time.

    d. Ease of indenture modification (relative to changing the terms of a public offering).

  2. Disadvantages:

    a. Relatively high interest costs.

    b. Large cash drain due to amortization payments.

    c. Restrictions on operations and higher credit standards which are insisted upon by lenders.

H. The use of term lending has broad implications for the entire economy, since term loans provide several advantages:

  1. Reduced vulnerability of the economy to forced liquidation.

  2. Movement of insurance firms (with their stable inflow of funds) into direct lending.

  3. A partial solution of the long-term debt problem of small business.

II. Conditional sales contracts.

A. Conditional sales contracts represent, in effect, long-term accounts receivable financing.

  1. The buyer purchases equipment and pays for it in installments over a one-to-five year period.

  2. Until payment is completed, the seller of the equipment continues to hold title to the equipment.

  3. Transference of the title is conditional upon satisfactory completion of the payments.

  4. The manufacturer or dealer sells the conditional sales contract to a bank or finance company.

    a. This agency holds title to the equipment until final payment is made.

    b. In case of a payment default, the financing agency repossesses the equipment and returns it to the manufacturer or dealer.

B. Generally, conditional sales contracts are used by small firms with low credit ratings.

C. The down payment required under such a sales contract is from 10-30 percent of the purchase price, and the payment period is related to the economic life of the equipment.

D. Costs are relatively high.

  1. The rate quoted is discounted from the face amount of the contract, resulting in an effective rate of interest of 14-15 percent.

2. On heavy machinery purchased by prime credit risks, the nominal rate may run as low as the prime rate with an effective rate of 8-9 percent.

E. Evaluation of conditional sales contracts:

  1. Advantages:

  a. Income from the equipment financed helps provide for repayment of the loan.

  b. High interest rates may be offset by profitability of equipment acquired.

  c. Ability of small firms to purchase equipment is increased.

  2. Limitations:

  a. Finances only a portion of fixed assets.

  b. Does not finance working capital.

III. Lease financing.

A. Major forms:

  1. *Sale and leaseback*—a firm owning land, buildings or equipment sells the property and simultaneously executes an agreement to lease the property for a specified period under specific terms.

  a. The seller receives the sale price of the property but retains the right to use it.

  b. Payments provided for by the lease are sufficient to return the full purchase price plus a stated return to the buyer.

  2. *Service leases* or *operating leases* include both financing and maintenance services.

  a. The lease contract is written for less than the expected life of the leased equipment.

  b. Such leases typically contain a cancellation clause permitting the lessee to cancel the lease and return the equipment before the expiration of the basic lease agreement.

  3. *Financial leases*—do not provide for maintenance services and are not cancellable.

  a. These leases provide for full amortization of cost, plus a return on the unamortized balance.

  b. Sale-leaseback is a special type of financial lease.

B. Annual lease payments are deductible for income tax purposes provided the following requirements stated by the Internal Revenue Service are included in the agreement:

  1. The term of the lease must be less than 30 years.

  2. The rental payment must provide a reasonable rate of return to the lessor.

  3. A renewal option is bona fide. A minimum requirement is that the lessee meet the best outside offer.

  4. There shall be no purchase option.

IV. Cost comparisons of lease financing with alternatives.

A. Lease cost is compared with a bank loan. Cash flow differentials are discounted at appropriate rates—cost of debt for most differentials, average cost of capital for salvage value.

B. Effects of accelerated depreciation.
   1. Initially, it would appear that the use of accelerated depreciation provides greater tax benefits to owning.
   2. However, the lessor will be forced by competition to share these benefits with the lessee, so the final result depends upon competitive conditions.
C. Interest rates are frequently assumed to be higher in leasing than in borrowing.
   1. But this may reflect higher risks to lessors than other lenders.
   2. It may be difficult to separate money costs and the cost of other specialist services provided by the lessor.
D. Residual property values:
   1. Rising real estate values favor the ownership of land and buildings.
   2. Obsolescence of equipment and low salvage values favor leasing such equipment.
E. Costs of obsolescence.
   1. Lessor bears costs of obsolescence, which would tend to favor leasing if obsolescence rate is high.
   2. But the lessor's reconditioning and marketing may enable it to find users for whom older equipment is still economical. This may reduce costs of obsolescence to both lessor and lessee.

PROBLEMS

16-1. Initially, the balance sheet of Holt Corporation shows a debt-assets ratio of 70 percent. It then leases a machine tool that has a cost equal to the amount of its original assets. What debt-assets ratio will the "postlease" balance sheet show if Holt does not capitalize the rental expense?

Solution:

No change. Holt is purchasing a service, not an asset, so the balance sheet will not be altered.

16-2. A firm has contracted to repay a term loan in ten annual installments of $300 each. If the interest rate is 8 percent, what is the amount of the loan?

Solution:

P.V. of annuity for 10 years at 8% = 6.710, (Table A-4)

$$R = \frac{An}{IF} \qquad \$300 = \frac{An}{6.710} \qquad An = \$2013$$

16-3. In the preceding problem what is the outstanding loan balance at the end of the *second* year?

Solution:

Year	Total payment	Interest payment	Loan repay	Balance
1	$300	$161	$139	$1874*
2	$300	$150	$150	$1724

* $1,874 = ($2,013 − $139)

16-4. A firm has recently expanded production and now requires a new machine tool. The firm's management is considering two alternative means of financing the machine—an outright purchase or financial lease (not cancellable). You have been asked to develop an analysis of the relative costs of owning versus leasing; which of the interest rates below will you use to determine the proper discount factor?
a. Cost of debt.
b. Cost of preferred dividends.
c. Cost of retained earnings.
d. Cost of equity.
e. Weighted average cost of capital.

Solution:

    a. The cost of debt is the appropriate choice since there is essentially no risk to the firm of obtaining the savings of the preferable alternative.

16-5. Assuming the terms of a particular lease option are not subject to change, which of the following would decrease the cost of owning?
a. The elimination of accelerated depreciation for tax purposes.
b. The introduction of the investment tax credit.
c. An increased salvage value.
d. An increased obsolescence rate.

Solution:

    b and c would both decrease the cost of owning.

16-6. Often, direct term loans issued by commercial banks can be distinguished from those issued by insurance companies. Which of the below are likely to be useful distinguishing characteristics?
a. Maturity of the loan.
b. Borrower's use of the funds.
c. Size of the loan.

d. Collateral on the loan.

e. Size of the borrower.

Solution:

All except b. The remaining choices typically indicate whether the loan was issued by a bank or insurance firm. As maturity, size of loan, collateral, and size of borrower increase, it is more likely the loan was offered by an insurance company.

16-7. Which of the following is an advantage of owning as opposed to leasing?

a. Protection against obsolescence.

b. Tax deductibility of the lease expense.

c. Protection against decline in salvage value.

d. Tax deductibility of depreciation expense.

e. Understatement of financial leverage on the balance sheet.

Solution:

d. However, the tax deductibility of the depreciation expense is offset by the tax deductibility of the lease expense.

16-8. The Town Department Store has been growing rapidly. Management estimates that it will need an additional $4 million during the next two years. Because of its weak current position, the store is considering the sale and leaseback of its land and building for $9 million. The annual net rental would be $600,000. The immediate use of the sales' proceeds will be to retire bank loans and mortgages. The current balance sheet and recent earnings are shown below.

Town Department Store–Balance sheet, December 31, 1972
(in millions of dollars)

Cash	$1		Accounts payable	$5
Receivables	7		Bank loans, 5%	5
Inventories	6		Other current debt	1
Total current assets		$14	Total current debt	$11
Land	$1		Mortgage on property, 5%	3
Buildings	4		Common stock	2
Equipment and fixtures	1		Retained earnings	4
Net fixed assets		6		
Total assets		$20	Total claims on assets	$20

Annual depreciation charges are $200,000 on the building and $400,000 on the equipment and fixtures. Profit before taxes in 1972 is $1,600,000; after taxes, $800,000.

a. How much capital gains tax will Town pay if the land and building are sold, and what are the net proceeds? (Assume all capital gains are taxed at the capital gains tax rate.)

b. If the lease had been in effect during 1972, what would Town's profit after taxes have been? (Assume a 50 percent tax rate.)

c. If the firm uses the net proceeds of the sale to reduce the bank loan and accounts payable instead of the mortgage, what will be its new current ratio?

d. List some advantages and disadvantages of the sale-and-leaseback operation, and recommend whether or not the firm should adopt the proposal.

Solution:

a.
Sale price	$9,000,000
Basis (land + building)	5,000,000
Capital gains	$4,000,000
Tax at 30%	1,200,000

Net proceeds = sales price − tax = $9,000,000 − $1,200,000
= $7,800,000

b.
Profit before taxes	$1,600,000
Add: interest on bank loans	250,000
interest on mortgage	150,000
depreciation on building	200,000
profit before taxes, interest and depreciation	$2,200,000
Less: rental	600,000
Taxable income	$1,600,000
Tax at 50%	800,000
Profit after taxes	$ 800,000

c.
Net proceeds	$7.8 million
Reduction in current liabilities	7.8 million
Total current debt ($11 million − $7.8 million)	3.2 million
New current ratio ($14 million/$3.2 million)	4.38 times

d. *Advantages.* Improves current position; opens the possibility for more borrowing from the bank in the future; increases the firm's ability to obtain funds; avoids restrictions in loan agreements.

Disadvantages. Leasing may have less flexibility than the alternatives; firm may lose benefits of increases in property values.

The lease is recommended. The firm can carry the fixed charges of the lease because of its high profitability. However, the firm is

underfinanced with equity money. It should plow back the high
profits to build up net worth and consider outside equity money.

16-9. The Brown Company is faced with the decision whether to purchase or to
lease a new fork-lift truck. The truck can be leased on a five-year contract
for $2,400 a year, or it can be purchased for $8,000. The lease includes
maintenance and service. The salvage value of the truck 5 years hence is
$2,000. The company uses the sum-of-the-years digits method of depreci-
ation. If the truck is owned, service and maintenance charges (a deductible
cost) would be *$400 a year.* The company can borrow at 10 percent for
amortized term loans. It has a 50 percent marginal tax rate, and the average after-tax cost of capital is 14 percent.
  a. Which method of acquiring the use of equipment should the company
     choose?
  b. Explain how you chose your discount rate or rates, emphasizing risk
     differentials and before-tax versus after-tax costs.

Solution:

  a. Amortization of loan.
     Present worth of 4 annual payments = $p \times$ [IF at 10% for 4 years,
                                  Table A-4]
                      $8,000 = $p \times$ [3.170]
                          p = $2,524, constant annual
                                  payment

Note: Solution a. is continued on page 156.

  b. We used the after-tax cost of debt for discounting all cash flows except
     the salvage value on the ground that these cash flows have about the
     same degree of certainty (variances around their expected value) as do
     interest payments.
       The salvage value, on the other hand, is more risky. We assume that it
     is about as risky as the average cash flow from operating assets, so we
     used the average after-tax cost of capital to discount the salvage value.
     All cash flows are on an after-tax basis, so to maintain consistency an
     after-tax discount rate should be employed.

Comparison of cost of leasing versus buying

(1) Year	(2) Loan payment	(3) Interest	(4) Repayment	(5) Balance	(6) Depreciation	(7) Service and maintenance costs	(8) (3)+(6)+(7) Tax expense	(9) ½X(8) Tax Savings	(10) (2)+(7)–(9) Net cost of owning	(11) Lease cost after tax	(12) (11)–(10) Advantage to owning	(13) 5% P.V. Factor table (A-2)	(14) (12)X(13) Value of advantage to owning
1	$2,524	$800	$1,724	$6,276	$2,400	$400	$3,600	$1,800	$1,124	$1,200	$ 76	0.952	$ 72
2	2,524	628	1,896	4,380	1,800	400	2,828	1,414	1,510	1,200	(310)	0.907	(281)
3	2,524	438	2,086	2,294	1,200	400	2,038	1,019	1,905	1,200	(705)	0.864	(609)
4	2,524	229	2,294	—	600	400	1,229	615	2,309	1,200	(1,109)	0.823	(913)
5	2,000*								(2,000)		2,000	0.592**	1,184
													$ (547)

Conclusion: The analysis favors the leasing alternative, since its net cost is lower than that of the purchase alternative.

* Salvage value

** p.v. factor, Table (A-2), 4 years, column of 14% = average after tax cost of capital.

Part VI
Long-Term Financing

Chapter 17

The Market for Long-Term Securities

Theme: The operation of the capital markets and the laws which regulate them influence the timing and use of long-term financing. The effective use of long-term financing has a major impact on the value of the firm because long-term financing decisions, like long-term investment decisions, can be altered only at substantial costs.

I. Capital markets.
  A. Investment bankers are the main intermediaries in the new issue market.
  B. Securities already issued are traded on securities exchanges and over-the-counter.

II. Organized security exchanges are physical entities operating as auction markets.
  A. Direct participation in these "auctions" is limited to individuals or representatives of organizations who buy "seats" on the exchange.
  B. Two practices said to contribute to effectively functioning securities markets are *margin trading* and *short selling*.
    1. Margin trading is the purchase of securities on credit. Limitations on credit purchases are set by the Federal Reserve Board.
    2. Short selling is the sale of securities not owned at time of sale in the expectation of a price decline.
    3. Effects of margin trading and short selling:
      a. They provide a more continuous market by increasing activity.
      b. They provide a more rapid price adjustment mechanism by increasing the flexibility of traders.
  C. Benefits of security exchanges to the economy are:
    1. Exchanges lower the cost of capital to businesses.
    2. Exchanges provide a continuous test of the values of securities.
    3. Exchanges increase the frequency of security price fluctuations and reduce the amplitude of their changes.
    4. Exchanges aid in the absorption of new issue flotations.

III. Over-the-counter security markets provide for security transactions not conducted on the organized exchanges.

A. In these markets brokers and dealers buy and sell securities into and out of their own inventories.

B. A comparison of trading in this market with trading in the organized exchanges shows:

1. The stocks of most companies are traded over-the-counter, but the stocks of larger firms are listed and two-thirds of the dollar volume of stock trading takes place through exchanges.

2. However, over 95 percent of bond transactions take place over the counter.

IV. In deciding whether to list his securities on an exchange, the financial manager weighs the following arguments:

A. Arguments for listing:

1. Public reporting of transactions advertises the firm.

2. Prestige and goodwill is obtained by providing the information required for listing.

3. Listed securities are more acceptable as loan collateral.

4. Supervision of transactions prevents manipulation.

B. Arguments against listing:

1. Over-the-counter dealers maintain a market and stimulate trading.

2. Over-the-counter dealers develop a market until a security is ready for listing.

3. It is more difficult to remove securities from listing than to list them; thus, to some degree, the decision is irreversible.

4. Over-the-counter stocks are subject to lower margin requirements than are listed securities.

5. More information on operations must be provided if stocks are listed.

V. Investment banking includes the following aspects:

A. *Public flotation* of a security issue is carried out through investment bankers who perform the following functions:

1. *Underwriting*—The investment banker purchases the new security issue, pays the issuer, and markets the securities. The banker bears the risk of price fluctuation from the time of purchase to the time that the issue is distributed.

2. *Distribution*—The investment banker maintains a sales staff which performs the marketing function.

3. *Advice and counsel*—The experience of the investment banker enables him to advise the issuer regarding the characteristics of the issue to ensure successful flotation. Often the banker serves on the board of directors in order to give advice and to protect his own reputation by securing sound management for the firm.

4. *Source of funds*—The investment banker provides a source of funds to the issuing firm during the distribution period.

B. The process of floating a public issue follows these steps:

1. *Preunderwriting conferences* are held between the issuing firm and the investment banker to discuss alternative forms of financing and to reach the decision to float an issue.
2. *An underwriting investigation* is made by the underwriters into the firm's prospects. Specialists are called in to examine legal, accounting, engineering, and other aspects of the firm.
3. The *underwriting agreement* is formulated and specifies, for example, the price of the issue to the public and the formation of an underwriting syndicate.
4. A *registration statement* is filed with the Securities and Exchange Commission. A minimum waiting period of 20 days is required before clearance by the Securities and Exchange Commission is received. The underwriter can make no sales during this time but can distribute preliminary prospectuses.
5. The price paid for securities by the underwriter is determined in the following manner:
    a. When a company "goes public" for the first time, the investment banker and the firm negotiate the price in accordance with valuation principles, and a final price is established at the close of the S.E.C. waiting period.
    b. When additional offerings are involved, the firm and the underwriter agree to price the securities in relation to the closing price on the last day of registration.
    c. Generally, the investment banker prefers a low price and a high yield, while the issuer of the securities naturally wants the opposite.
6. An underwriting syndicate may be formed by the investment banker for these reasons:
    a. To reduce the extent of his risk.
    b. To use the selling organizations of other investment bankers.
    c. He may be unable to finance a large issue by himself.
7. A *selling group* is a group of dealers who act as retailers of the issue. The operations of the group are governed by an agreement which covers these points:
    a. Description of the issue.
    b. Price concession, which is the selling group's commission.
    c. Handling of repurchased securities. (Note: The syndicate manager takes subscriptions until the issue is sold. He also stabilizes the market while the books are open in order to facilitate the placement of the issue.)
    d. Duration of the selling group.
C. Analysis of the costs of public flotations shows these relationships:
    1. Ranking of costs from highest to lowest:
        a. Common stock.
        b. Preferred stock.
        c. Debt.

This ranking is explained by the larger marketing task for stock flotations, since this market is narrower than the debt market.

2. Costs as a percentage of the proceeds of the issue are greater for small than for large issues. Fixed expenses are high, and the selling job and risks are greater for the securities of small firms.

D. The role of the investment banker is not limited to his traditional functions of handling issues. He has extended his activities in these fields:

1. The procurement of risk capital for new enterprises.
2. Acting as a broker for private placements.
3. The organization of investment trusts.
4. Acting as a middleman in merger negotiations.
5. Contracting to maintain the market for rights during the trading period.

VI. Regulation of security trading.

A. The financial manager should be aware of the federal laws regulating issuance and trading of securities because they influence his liability and affect financing costs.

B. The Securities Act of 1933 relates to the marketing of new issues. It seeks to provide full disclosure of information, a record of representations, and penalties for violations. The major provisions are:

1. The Act applies to public interstate offerings over $300,000 (subject to certain exceptions).
2. It requires registration 20 days in advance of the offering to the public.
3. It allows purchasers who suffer loss due to misrepresentation or omission of material facts to sue for damages.

C. The Securities Exchange Act of 1934 extends the disclosure principle to the trading of existing issues. Its major provisions are:

1. The Act establishes the S.E.C. (Securities and Exchange Commission).
2. It requires registration and regulation of the national securities exchanges.
3. It requires corporate insiders to file monthly reports of changes in ownership of stock of the corporation and provides legal redress for stockholders.
4. It gives the S.E.C. power to prohibit manipulations through wash sales, pools, and pegging operations.
5. It gives the S.E.C. control over proxy machinery and practices.
6. It gives the Board of Governors of the Federal Reserve System power to determine margin requirements.

D. The Maloney Act of 1938 provides for self-regulation of securities brokers and dealers, and this resulted in the formation of the National Association of Securities Dealers.

E. The Bankruptcy Act of 1938 was a general revision of federal bankruptcy law. It requires the courts to seek advisory opinions from the S.E.C. in cases which involve liabilities over $3 million.

F. The Investment Company Act of 1940 has the following provisions:

1. It seeks to prevent investment fund managers from:
   a. Using excessive leverage.
   b. Making speculative investments.
   c. Taking excessive fees and salaries.
2. Its major provisions regarding investment companies include:
   a. Registration with the S.E.C. is required.
   b. An investment company cannot own in excess of 10 percent of a corporation's stock.
   c. Their capital structures are regulated.
   d. Uniform accounting methods and periodic reports to stockholders are prescribed.

PROBLEMS

17-1. Margin trading is the process of _____.

Solution:

Buying securities on credit.

17-2. When an investor is buying on margin, the securities are:
   a. Delivered to the buyer within the next four business days.
   b. Held by the brokerage house.
   c. Delivered to the exchange for certification.
   d. Retained by the seller.
   e. None of the above.

Solution:

b.

17-3. A member of an exchange who is responsible for maintaining an "orderly market" is known as _____.

Solution:

A specialist.

17-4. True or false? The Securities Exchange Commission determines margin requirements.

Solution:

False. The Board of Governors of the Federal Reserve determines margin requirements.

17-5. True or false? Most bond issues are traded in the over-the-counter market.

Solution:

True.

17-6. Securities flotation costs increase as one moves from bonds to preferred stock, and then to common stock. What best explains this phenomenon?

Solution:

Large block purchases of bonds by institutions.

Theme: To utilize the various forms of financing effectively, the financial manager must be aware of the ramifications of using each form. This chapter describes in some detail the typical provisions of common stock financing.

I. Income and control differs among the various forms of ownership.
  A. Individual proprietorships:
    1. When funded entirely by the owner, all rights to income, control, and responsibility for debt lie with the owner.
    2. When funded at least in part through debt, limitations are placed on control and the apportionment of income.
  B. Partnership rights are apportioned by agreement or by state law.
  C. Business corporation rights are apportioned by the state of incorporation and are set forth in the corporate charter.
II. Owners of common stock in business corporations have these general rights:
  A. Collective rights:
    1. Make charter amendments if the changes are approved by state officials.
    2. Adopt and amend the bylaws.
    3. Elect the corporate directors.
    4. Authorize the sale of fixed assets.
    5. Ratify mergers.
    6. Change the amount of authorized common stock.
    7. Authorize issuance of securities.
  B. Each stockholder also has specific rights as an individual owner enabling him to:
    1. Vote as prescribed by the corporate charter.
    2. Transfer stock to another party.
    3. Inspect the books of the corporation.
    4. Share in the residual assets in case of dissolution.
  C. Apportionment of income and control.
    1. Common stock is the recipient of the residual income of the corporation.

2. Through the right to vote, holders of common stock have legal control of the corporation.
  a. Each stockholder has the right to cast votes in proportion to the number of shares he owns.
    1. A *proxy* is a transfer of the right to vote.
    2. The use of proxies is supervised by the Securities and Exchange Commission to prevent:
    a. Self-perpetuation of management.
    b. Small stockholder groups from gaining special advantages.
  b. In *cumulative voting* the stockholder is allowed to cast multiple votes for one director. For example, 100 shares can be cast as 500 votes for one director if five directors are being elected, rather than 100 votes for each of five directors.
    1. Formula:

$$r = \frac{d \times S}{D + 1} + 1$$

  where
    r = number of shares required to elect a desired number of directors
    d = number of directors desired to elect
    S = total number of shares of common stock outstanding and entitled to vote
    D = total number of directors to be elected.
    2. Illustration:
    $d = 2$
    $S = 100,000$
    $D = 6$

$$r = \frac{2 \times 100,000}{6 + 1} + 1 = 28,572$$

  c. The *preemptive right* gives the existing equity owners the option to purchase any additional new issues of common stock.
    1. State laws vary with regard to the preemptive right.
    a. In some states it is a part of every corporate charter.
    b. In other states it must be included as a specific provision.
    2. The preemptive right is designed to protect:
    a. The power of control.
    b. The pro rata share of earned surplus and earning power for the present stockholders.
  d. With regard to risk:
    1. Common stockholders have limited liability in the case of loss.
    2. Common equity provides a cushion for creditors if losses occur on dis-

solutions. The equity-to-total assets ratio is an indicator of the degree by which the amounts realized on the liquidation of assets may decline from stated book values before creditors suffer losses.

III. Common stock financing.

  A. In reaching a decision to issue common stock, the financial manager should consider these factors:

    1. Advantages of common stock over other forms of financing.

      a. No fixed charges are incurred.

      b. There is no maturity date.

      c. The credit worthiness of the firm is increased.

    2. Disadvantages of common stock.

      a. The control of the firm is shared with the new shareholders.

      b. The new shares participate fully in earnings and dividends.

      c. Flotation costs are relatively high.

      d. Stock normally sells on a higher yield basis than debt.

      e. Dividends are not deductible from income for tax purposes.

    3. Circumstances favoring the use of common stock.

      a. The firm's sales and profits fluctuate widely.

      b. Profit margins do not cover the cost of debt.

      c. The firm already has a high debt ratio in relation to the prudent maximum for its line of business.

      d. The firm is new, lacking access to debt financing.

      e. Dilution of control is not a problem.

      f. Cash flow considerations are important.

      g. The relative costs of common stock financing appear favorable.

      h. Available debt financing would carry onerous loan agreement restrictions.

      i. Investors, perhaps worried by the threat of inflation, favor equity to debt securities at the present time. (This point is discussed in detail in Chapter 23.)

  B. The use of rights in financing.

    1. Definitions:

      a. A *right* is an option to buy a part of newly issued stock at a specified price during a designated period of time.

      b. A *rights offering* involves the sale of additional stock to existing stockholders, and is mandatory if the preemptive right exists for the firm in question.

      c. The *oversubscription privilege* contained in most rights offerings allows stockholders to buy on a pro rata basis all shares not taken in the initial offering. This privilege also helps to assure a full sale of the new stock issue.

    2. Considerations affecting the financial manager's decision to make a rights offering:

      a. There are three major alternative methods of selling stock:

1. Alternative I—sell the issue through investment bankers with or without rights.
   a. Advantages.
      1. Wide distribution of shares.
      2. Certainty of receiving the funds.
   b. Disadvantages—the relatively high cost of the underwriter's services.
2. Alternative II – issue rights but provide only a small discount from market price (and use investment bankers to sell unsubscribed shares).
   a. Advantages.
      1. Smaller underwriting expense.
      2. Small decrease in unit price of shares.
   b. Disadvantage—somewhat narrower distribution of shares.
3. Alternative III—issue rights, allow a large discount and do not use investment banking facilities.
   a. Advantages.
      1. No underwriting expense.
      2. Substantial decrease in the unit price of shares.
   b. Disadvantages.
      1. Pressure on owners to exercise rights.
      2. Narrower distribution of shares.
   b. The choice of method depends on the individual company's needs.
3. Several questions face the financial manager in a rights offering:
   a. How many rights will be required to purchase a share of the new stock?
   b. What should be the value of each right?
   c. What effect will the rights offering have on the price of the existing stock?
   d. What will be the subscription price of the stock?
4. To determine the number of rights required to purchase a new share of stock:
   a. Calculate the number of new shares. (Number of new shares = funds to be raised/subscription price.)
   b. Calculate the number of rights needed to buy a new share:

Number of rights required = number of old shares/number of new shares.

5. To determine the value of each right, the following formulas may be used:

$$R = \frac{M_o - S}{N + 1} \quad \text{(Rights-on-calculation)}$$

$$R = \frac{M_e - S}{N} \quad \text{(Ex-rights calculation)}$$

where R = value of one right

M_O = rights-on price of the stock

M_e = ex-rights price of the stock

S = subscription price

N = number of rights required to purchase one share.

    a. Stock is sold rights-on until a predetermined ex-rights day.

    b. The ex-rights value of the stock differs from the rights-on value of the stock by the value of a right as determined in the above equation.

6. If a stockholder exercises or sells his rights, a rights offering does not affect the value of his stock. However, a stockholder may suffer a loss if:

    a. He forgets to exercise or sell his rights.

    b. Brokerage costs of selling the rights are excessive.

7. A company may feel that a rights offering has a higher probability of raising funds without lowering the market price of stock because:

    a. If existing shareholders wish to maintain their pro rata share in the earnings and control of the firm, they will exercise their rights.

    b. Existing shareholders are most likely to have a favorable opinion of the firm.

    c. Margin requirements on rights purchases are only 25 percent as compared to 65 percent for regular stock purchases.

8. Some observed differences between market price and subscription price include:

    a. From 1946-1957, subscription prices were about 25 percent less than market prices.

    b. Subscription prices have been about 15 percent lower than market prices in recent years.

    c. Generally, subscription prices are from 10 percent to 20 percent lower than market prices.

9. No generalization can be made regarding the effects of a rights offering on the market price of the stock; the effect of the offering depends upon the market's evaluation of the future prospects of the issuing company.

PROBLEMS

18-1. Bigham Corporation needs $30 million in new outside equity funds. The current market price of its stock is $50 per share, and it is selling at ten times earnings. If current earnings are $40 million and the subscription price is set at $30, what is the value of one right?

Solution:

$$\frac{\$50 \text{ price}}{10 \text{ P/E}} = \$5 \text{, EPS}$$

$$\frac{\$40,000,000 \text{ earnings}}{\$5 \text{ EPS}} = 8,000,000 \text{ old shares}$$

$$\frac{\$30,000,000 \text{ new equity needed}}{\$30 \text{ subscription price}} = 1,000,000 \text{ new shares needed}$$

$$\frac{8,000,000}{1,000,000} = 8 \text{ rights per new share}$$

$$R = \frac{M_O - S}{N + 1} = \frac{\$50 - \$30}{8 + 1} = \frac{20}{9} = \$2.22 \text{, value of one right}$$

18-2. Ajax Corporation's three million shares of common stock are currently selling at a market price of $50 per share. The firm plans to raise an additional $20 million through rights by selling 500,000 new shares of stock at $40 per share. a) What will be the theoretical price of the common stock after the financing is completed? b) What is the theoretical value of one right?

Solution:

a.   3,000,000, current shares
            X $50, market price
    $150,000,000, market value of firm
     +20,000,000, additional funds to be raised
    $170,000,000, total value of firm after rights issue

    $ 3,000,000, current shares outstanding
        +500,000, new shares
    $ 3,500,000, total shares outstanding after rights issue

$$\frac{\$170,000,000}{3,500,000} = \$48.57 \text{ theoretical price}$$

b. $\dfrac{3,000,000}{500,000} = 6$ rights per share

$$R = \frac{M_O - S}{r + 1} = \frac{\$50 - \$40}{7} = \frac{10}{7} = \$1.43$$

18-3. Assume you owned 30 shares of stock before the rights offering. How much better off is your financial position if you do exercise your rights (rather than sell)?

Solution:

No change. Whether or not rights are exercised or sold leaves the net present wealth of the stockholder unchanged. This is insured by the arbitrage operations of the market. It is true even when commission costs are taken into account.

18-4. ABC Corporation needs additional funds and has three alternatives open to it. It can:

a. Sell stock at the current market price using investment bankers (ABC will net 95 percent of the market price).

b. Sell stock using rights through investment bankers (using a subscription price set at 85 percent of the market price).

c. Sell stock using rights without utilizing investment bankers (using a subscription price set at 15 percent of the market price).

Which alternative (or alternatives) should ABC adopt if it wishes to minimize the reduction in market price per share?

Solution:

a. Choose (a), because there is a "stock dividend effect" in any successful rights offering which tends to lower the market price per share.

18-5. The Broadway Company is financed solely with common stock. Its balance sheet is given below.

Earnings available to common stock after taxes are $30,000. The price-earnings ratio is 16, so the current market price is $48 per share ($3 × 16).

Broadway Company – Balance sheet, end of year, 1972

		Common stock	
		(10,000 shares)	$ 30,000
		Surplus	120,000
Total assets	$150,000	Total claims	$150,000

The company sells an additional 10,000 shares at $25 per share with a rights offering whereby one new share can be purchased for each old share held.

New balance sheet

		Common stock, $3 par	$ 60,000
		Capital surplus	220,000
		Surplus	120,000
Total assets	$400,000	Total claims	$400,000

After the rights offering has been completed and the assets obtained have become productive, earnings available to common stock after taxes go up to $80,000.

a. What is the value of each right?

b. What will be the new market price of the stock when it goes ex-rights if the market price of the stock falls by the value of one right?

c. What will be the new market price of the stock if the same price-earnings ratio prevails before and after the rights offering?

Solution:

a. $R = \dfrac{M_O - S}{N + 1} = \dfrac{48 - 25}{1 + 1} = \dfrac{23}{2} = \$11.50$

b. $\$48 - \$11.50 = \$36.50$

c. Earnings per share times P/E ratio
$\$4.00 \times 16 = \$64.00$

18-6. Robert Roos has 200 shares of Eastern Industries. The market price per share is $70. The company now offers stockholders one new share to be purchased at $52 for every five shares held.

a. Determine the value of each right.

b. Assume that Robert (1) uses 75 rights and sells the other 125, or (2) sells the 200 rights at the market price you have calculated.

Prepare a statement showing the changes in his position under the above assumptions.

Solution:

a. $\dfrac{M_O - S}{N + 1} = \dfrac{\$70 - \$52}{5 + 1} = \dfrac{\$18}{6} = \$3 \text{ per right}$

b. 1.

Original holdings		Market value of	
(200 shares at $70)	$14,000	215* shares at $67	$14,405
Use of 75 rights		Gain on sale of	
(15 shares at $52)	780	125 rights at $3	375
Total investment	$14,780	Stockholder position	$14,780

2.

Original holdings		Market value of	
(200 shares at $70)	$14,000	200 shares at $67	$13,400
Total investment	$14,000	Gain on sale of	
		200 rights at $3	600
		Stockholder position	$14,000

*The 75 rights are exercised into 15 new shares. Total shares = new 15 + old 200 = 215 shares.

18-7. You are a dissident stockholder of Baler Corporation and have collected 20 percent of the 100,000 voting shares outstanding. If a total of seven directors are to be elected to the board, how many directors can you elect, assuming cumulative voting is used?

Solution:

$$r = \frac{D \times S}{D + 1} + 1 \quad or \quad D = \frac{(r - 1)(D + 1)}{S}$$

$$D = \frac{19,999 \times 8}{100,000} = \frac{159,992}{100,000} = 1.60$$

1 director.

18-8. A firm with 300,000 shares of stock outstanding—market price $15 per share—decided to raise additional funds through a new equity issue. After the issue was sold, total shares outstanding doubled, and the market value of the firm rose to $8 million. At what price was the new stock sold? (Ignore flotation costs.)

Solution:

a. $\underline{\quad\quad 300,000}$, shares
$\underline{\quad\quad \times \$15}$, price per share
$\$4,500,000$, market value

b. $\$8,000,000$, market value after new funds
$\underline{-4,500,000}$, market value before new funds
$\$3,500,000$, market value of new funds

c. $\dfrac{\$3,500,000 \text{ market value of new funds}}{300,000 \text{ new shares}} = \$11.67$, price of new share

18-9. If ABC Corporation has 8,000 shares of common stock outstanding, and the balance sheet given below, what is the book value of the common stock?

Balance sheet

		Payables	$ 2,500
		Loans	47,500
		Mortgages	100,000
		Preferred stock	100,000
		Common stock	400,000
		Capital surplus	50,000
		Earned surplus	50,000
		Total liabilities and	
Total assets	$750,000	capital	$750,000

Solution:

a. $400,000, common stock
   50,000, capital surplus
   50,000, earned surplus
   $500,000

b. $\dfrac{\$500,000}{8,000 \text{ shares}} = \$62.50$, book value of common stock

18-10. Pacific Air Lines, Inc., provides transcontinental service throughout the United States. In 1972, Pacific's domestic services were fifth in size among airlines of the United States. The company was seeking to raise $10 million for general corporate purposes. Relevant financial information is given in the balance sheet. The data have been altered slightly.

Pacific Airlines, Inc.—Balance sheet, June 30, 1971
(in millions of dollars)

Cash	$ 13.0	Accounts payable	$ 14.0
U.S. Government securities	4.0	Notes payable	6.0
Receivables	15.0	Accruals	10.0
Supplies	2.0		
Other current assets	1.0	Total current liabilities	$ 30.0
		Long-term debt	90.0
Total current assets	$ 35.0	Total debt	$120.0
Net property	113.0	Common stock, par $3:	
Other assets	2.0	Outstanding: 1.5	
		million shares	4.5
		Capital surplus	15.0
		Retained earnings	10.5
		Net worth	$ 30.0
Total assets	$150.0	Total claims on assets	$150.0

Income data
(in millions of dollars)

	1971	1970	1969	1968
Sales	$150	$120	$104	$88
Earnings after tax available to common	4.50	3.00	4.00	1.00
Earnings per share	3.00	1.80	2.70	0.60
Dividends per share	0.90	0.90	0.45	0.70

Commercial Airlines Financial Ratios

Current ratio (X)	1.4
Sales to total assets (X)	0.9
Sales to inventory (X)	23.0
Average collection period (days)	38

Income data (continued)

Current debt/total assets (%)	15-20
Long-term debt/total assets (%)	50-55
Preferred/total assets (%)	0-5
Net worth/total assets (%)	25-30
Profits to sales (%)	2.6
Profits to total assets (%)	2.4
Profits to net worth (%)	7.5
Expected growth rate for earnings and dividends	7.0

Common stock could be sold for $45 per share. Sinking fund debentures (ten-year life) could be sold to yield 6 percent. Flotation costs would not be sufficient to affect the decision. Which form of financing should Pacific Air Lines use to raise the $10 million?

This question should not be answered in terms of precise cost of capital calculations. Rather, a more qualitative and subjective analysis is appropriate. The only calculations necessary are a few simple ratios. Careful interpretation of these ratios is necessary, however, to understand and discuss the often complex, subjective judgment issues involved.

Solution:

The following factors will be considered in the analysis:
a. Relative costs of the financing alternatives:

Price-earnings ratio $\dfrac{\$45}{\$3} = 15$ times

Earnings yield $\dfrac{\$3}{\$45} = 6.7\%$

Dividend yield $\dfrac{\$0.90}{\$45} = 2.0\%$

Estimated cost of retained earnings $k = \dfrac{D}{P} + g = 2.0\% + 7.0\%$

$$= 9.0\%$$

Cost of debt before tax 6%; 3% after tax

There is some cost advantage to debt, but the earnings yield is also quite low.
b. Level and stability of profits:

Profits to total assets $\dfrac{\$4.5}{\$150} = 3.0\%$

Profits to net worth $\dfrac{\$4.5}{\$30.0} = 15\%$

Profits to sales $\dfrac{\$4.5}{\$150} = 3.0\%$

Profits and earnings per share have been fluctuating a great deal, and the greater risk involved in a debt financing situation could present problems in meeting fixed costs and even lead to insolvency. Note that the earnings rate on net worth is 6.7 percent, compared with the profit rate on book net worth of 15 percent. The earnings rate on total assets is nearly that of the after-tax rate on debt financing, illustrating again the slim margin involved with debt financing.

c. Pacific Air Lines' current debt-total asset ratio is almost equal to the norm for the industry, but its long-term debt ratio is considerably higher. The pro forma statement (below) shows the further consequences of debt versus equity alternatives. With a debt issue the total debt percentage rises to 12 percent above the industry average. The equity alternative, on the contrary, brings Pacific's ratios more in line with those of the industry. Even so, the total debt ratio is 5 percent above the norm. This reinforces the argument for equity financing.

Percentage of total assets

			Pro forma	
	Industry	*Pacific*	*Debt*	*Equity*
Current debt	20%	20%	19%	19%
Long-term debt	50	60	62.5	56
Total debt	70	80	81.5	75
Preferred stock	0-5	0	0	0
Net worth	30	20	18.5	25

d. Sinking fund requirement (cash flows): The fact that the company must provide for a sinking fund on the debt alternative is another disadvantage from the corporate standpoint. To retire the bonds over a ten-year life means a 10 percent rate, plus the 3 percent interest cost, which amounts to 13 percent a year, or $1.3 million. There is little doubt that the common stock alternative is superior from a cash flow standpoint. This is true even with the added dividend payments created by the issuance of over 220,000 new shares. Assuming a $1 dividend, this added cash outlay amounts to only 17 percent of the outlay required under the debt alternative.

e. Dilution of control to present stockholders: Pacific Air Lines is a fairly well-established firm incorporated in 1930, and its 1.5 million shares are widely held. Thus, the additional 222,222 shares required to finance the equity issue will not present a dilution of control problem.

In conclusion, the common stock issue is favored. Actually, common stock was sold according to the company's prospectus of April 2, 1972.

Chapter 19

Fixed Income Securities: Debt and Preferred Stock

Theme: This chapter provides the financial manager with the technical materials to analyze debt decisions and to formulate financial policies regarding the use of alternative methods of obtaining financial leverage.

I. Some key definitions include the following:

A. A *bond* is a long-term promissory note.

B. A *mortgage* is a pledge of real assets as security for a loan.

C. A *debenture* is unsecured long-term debt.

D. *Funded debt* is any long-term debt.

E. An *indenture* is a document which contains the details of the long-term contractual relationship between the issuing corporation and the bondholders. It includes:

1. The form of the bond.

2. A description of any pledged property.

3. The authorized amount of the issue.

4. Protective clauses or covenants such as limitations on indebtedness, restrictions on dividends, or the minimum current ratio requirement during the period of bonded indebtedness.

5. Provisions for redemption or call privileges.

F. The *trustee* is an agent of the bondholders, but he is appointed by the issuer before the bonds are sold.

G. A *call provision* gives the issuing corporation the right to call the bond for redemption.

1. If used, the company must pay a call premium over and above the par value of the bond.

2. Since this provision is valuable to the firm but detrimental to an investor, interest rates on new issues of callable bonds exceed those on new issues of noncallable bonds.

H. A *sinking fund* facilitates the orderly retirement of a bond issue or preferred stock issue.

    1. Nature of sinking fund requirements:
      a. The firm is required to buy and retire a portion of the bond issue each year.
      b. The amount is sometimes related to the level of sales or earnings of the current year.
      c. Usually the requirement is a mandatory fixed amount.
      d. If mandatory, failure to meet a sinking fund payment usually constitutes a default on the bond issue.
    2. Alternative procedures for handling sinking funds:
      a. The sinking fund may be used to call a certain percentage of the bonds at a stipulated price, with bonds selected by lottery from serial numbers.
      b. The sinking fund payment may be used to buy bonds on the open market.
      c. The firm will choose the method that results in the greatest reduction of indebtedness for a given expenditure.
    3. The call provision of the sinking fund can work to the detriment of bondholders since the call is generally at par while the bond may have been purchased well above par.
    4. Since a sinking fund provides additional protection to investors, bonds that have them are likely to carry lower yields than comparable bonds with no sinking fund provisions.

II. Long-term debt can be classified on three bases:
  A. Priority of claims.
    1. A *senior mortgage* has first claim on assets and earnings.
    2. A *junior mortgage* has a subordinate lien.
    3. An *underlying mortgage* is a small senior mortgage with a lien prior to a large junior mortgage.
    4. *Subordinated debt* is unsecured debt, which is junior to others.
  B. Right to issue additional securities.
    1. A *closed-end mortgage* specifies that no additional bonds may be sold which have a lien on the property specified in the original mortgage.
    2. An *open-end mortgage* exists if the bond indenture fails to mention additional bond issues. Therefore, the property can be repledged.
    3. A *limited open-end mortgage* allows the sale of a specified amount of additional bonds.
  C. The factors given above have important influences on:
    1. The degree of protection for the creditor.
    2. The rate of interest paid by the firm.
    3. The rating of the bond by rating agencies.

III. Unsecured long-term debt.
  A. *Debentures* are unsecured bonds which are issued:
    1. When the firm's property is unsuitable for a lien.
    2. When the firm's finances are very strong.

3. When the firm is too weak to have alternatives.

B. *Income* bonds are bonds which pay interest only if the interest is earned.

1. In the past, they arose from reorganizations.

2. In recent years, they have been used in normal financing to replace a preferred stock issue because of the tax advantage of interest over dividends.

3. They typically contain:

   a. A cumulative provision.

   b. A sinking fund provision.

   c. Voting rights upon default of a specified number of interest payments.

C. *Subordinated debentures* are unsecured bonds that place the debenture below present and future senior debt with regard to priorities.

1. Advantages.

   a. Subordination strengthens the position of the senior creditors.

   b. Debentures have a tax advantage over preferred stock.

2. Finance companies are high leverage operations with debt-to-equity ratios, including subordinated debt, of around three to one.

3. For industrials, a rule of thumb requires firms to maintain an equity-to-subordinated-debt ratio of 150 to 200 percent.

D. A general principle of finance is that new forms of financing will be developed in order to meet changes in the needs of firms related to changes in the economic environment.

IV. Appraisal of long-term debt.

A. Advantages.

1. Debt has a limited cost.

2. Stockholders retain voting control.

3. Interest expense is tax deductible.

4. Provision for calling the debt adds flexibility to the financial structure.

B. Disadvantages.

1. A fixed interest commitment is made.

2. A definite maturity date exists requiring repayment or refunding.

3. Forecasting errors may lead to overcommitments.

4. Stringent indenture provision may be imposed.

5. Financial standards limit the amount of debt in the liability structure.

C. Decisions to use debt are favored by the following:

1. Sales and earnings are relatively stable.

2. Profit margins are adequate.

3. A rise in profits or the general price level is expected.

4. The existing debt ratio is relatively low.

5. Common stock price-earnings ratios are low.

6. Control considerations are important.

7. Cash flow requirements under the bond agreement are not burdensome.

8. Restrictions of the bond indenture are not onerous.

V. Preferred stock.

A. Under some circumstances, the financial manager will decide that preferred stock is a suitable source of funds because it limits cash payout and provides financial leverage.

B. Preferred stock is by nature a hybrid security. It is classed as debt or equity depending upon the analysis being made.

1. Preferred stock is *not* like equity (but *is* like debt) in that it does not carry voting rights.

2. Preferred stock is *not* like debt (but *is* like equity) in that failure to pay dividends does not cause default on the obligation.

C. The risks of preferred shareholders in relation to the risks of equity owners are reduced by these features:

1. Preferreds have prior claims to earnings and to assets in liquidation.

2. Occasionally, a sinking fund provides for the retirement of the issue.

3. Ordinarily, consent of the preferred shareholders must be obtained before securities with equal or prior claim on earnings can be issued.

4. Common stock dividends are restricted if the current ratio, debt ratio, or surplus account falls below prescribed limits.

VI. Major provisions.

A. Preferred dividend provisions.

1. The dividend may be stated as a percentage of the par value of the stock or as an annual dollar amount.

2. Preferreds are normally nonparticipating.

3. They are usually cumulative, so a preferred dividend which is passed is still owed.

a. To protect preferred holders, all preferred dividend arrearages must be paid before any common dividends are paid.

b. No interest is paid upon arrearages.

B. Other provisions:

1. About 40 percent of the preferred stock issued in recent years has been convertible into common stock.

2. For nonvoting issues, the right to vote is usually given upon the failure of the firm to pay dividends for six, eight, or ten quarters.

3. About 25 percent of preferred issues carry the preemptive right.

4. Some preferred issues have sinking fund and call provisions. When used, a call premium must be paid.

5. Most preferreds have no maturity date.

C. Summary of usual preferred stock provisions:

1. It is nonparticipating.

2. It is nonvoting.

3. It has a prior claim on earnings and assets.

4. It is cumulative.

5. It has no maturity.

6. It is callable.

VII. Appraisal.
  A. Advantages to the use of preferred stock:
    1. The obligation to make fixed payments is avoided.
    2. Obtains higher earnings for original owners if leverage is successful.
    3. Usually does not dilute existing control of the firm.
    4. Since it usually has no maturity and no sinking fund, it is more flexible than bonds.
    5. Enables the firm to conserve mortgageable assets.
  B. Disadvantages to the use of preferred stock:
    1. Sells at a higher yield than bonds.
    2. Dividends are not an expense for tax purposes.
VIII. Decision-making in the use of preferred stock.
  A. Since it is a hybrid security type, the use of preferred stock is favored by conditions that fall between those favoring the use of common stock and those favoring the use of debt.
    1. If profit margins are adequate, the firm will gain from the additional leverage provided by preferred stock.
    2. Relative costs of alternative sources of financing are important.
    3. When the use of debt involves excessive risk and the issuance of common stock poses control problems, preferred stock may be a good compromise.
  B. Recent trends in the use of preferred stock.
    1. Convertible preferred is used in connection with mergers.
      a. Use of cash or bonds in payment to the shareholders of the acquired company would constitute realized gains from a tax standpoint.
      b. If convertible preferred stock is paid to the selling stockholders, this constitutes a tax-free exchange of securities.
      c. Selling stockholders thus obtain a fixed income security while postponing the capital gains taxes.
    2. To avoid the tax disadvantage of nondeductibility of preferred stock dividends, companies have made exchange offers.
      a. Total securities offered exceeds the market value of the preferred.
      b. A common formula is to offer bonds equal in market value to the preferred, plus cash or common stock as extra inducement.
  C. Refunding a bond or preferred stock issue involves these points:
    1. A refunding operation involves the sale of a new issue of lower-yield securities. Proceeds from this sale are used to retire bonds or preferred stocks sold earlier at higher interest rates.
    2. Costs of refunding include:
      a. The call premium paid for the privilege of calling the old issue.
      b. The flotation costs involved in selling the new issue.
    3. Annual benefits of the refunding operation are equal to the difference in the interest payments associated with the old issue and the issue replacing it.

4. To determine whether refunding will be beneficial to the firm:
   a. Find the present value of the interest savings by discounting at the *after-tax* cost of the debt, then
   b. Compare this discounted value with the cash outlays associated with the refunding.

PROBLEMS

19-1. The preferred stock of the Cameron Corporation has a cumulative annual dividend of $1.00. In the six-year period of 1967 through 1972, the firm retained 100 percent of its earnings (paid no preferred dividends). If projected earnings after tax but before preferred dividends for 1972 are $125,000, what is the largest common dividend that could be paid out of current earnings? (Shares outstanding, 1967-1972: 10,000 preferred; 15,000 common.)

Solution:

$1.00, cumulative annual dividend
 X6, years (1967-1972)
$6.00, total cumulative dividend due

 10,000, shares preferred
  X$6
$60,000

$125,000, earnings
 60,000, preferred dividends due
$ 65,000, available for common dividends

$$\frac{\$65,000}{15,000} = \$4.33, \text{largest possible common dividend}$$

 19-2. Moulton Corporation has one million shares of $50 par value preferred stock outstanding. Which of the following is a reasonable call price for such an issue (*not* a call for sinking fund purposes)?
   a. $47.50   d. $65.00
   b. $50.00   e. all the above
   c. $55.00

Solution:

   c. Call prices are always set at some premium above par value.

19-3. Which combination of current ratio and debt ratio below would preferred stockholders prefer?

	Current ratio	Debt ratio
a.	Low	Low
b.	Low	High
c.	High	Low
d.	High	High

Solution:

    c. High current ratio—more liquid
       Low debt ratio—less risky

19-4. What is the major reason that many firms have retired their preferred stock?

Solution:

    The nondeductibility of dividends for tax purposes.

19-5. Given the balance sheet below, what percentage of the bank's claims will be satisfied if $500 is available for claims on liquidation?

Balance sheet

Bank debt	$ 600
Accounts payable	300
Subordinated debt (subordinated *only* to bank loan)	300
Common stock	2,000
Retained earnings	400
Total assets = $3,600 Total	$3,600

Solution:

Total debt = $1,200

	Initial position	Initial percentage	Initial distribution	Final distribution
Bank debt	$600/1200	0.50	$250	$375
Accounts payable	300/1200	0.25	125	125
Subordinated debt	300/1200	0.25	125	—
		1.00	$500	$500

$$\frac{\$375}{\$600} = 62.5\%$$

19-6. A firm has a $30 million bond issue outstanding. It carries a 6 percent
coupon and will be outstanding for ten years. The bond can be called at a
5 percent premium. The firm has an opportunity to float a new ten-year
bond issue of $30 million with a 4 percent coupon. It is predicted that
market interest rates will not fall below 4 percent. If flotation costs on
the new issue are $1,500,000, and tax effects are ignored, should the firm
refund the old bond and issue the new one? What is the net present value
of savings?

Solution:

Call premium: $30,000,000 × 0.05 = $1,500,000
Flotation costs: =   1,500,000
Total costs   = $3,000,000
Old interest payments: $30,000,000 × 0.06 = $1,800,000
New interest payments: $30,000,000 × 0.04 =   1,200,000
    Annual saving $ 600,000

P.V. of annuity 10 years at 4 percent, Table A-4
        8.111 × $600,000 = $4,866,600

                  $4,866,600
                  −3,000,000
Net present value $1,866,600

Since the net present value is positive, the refunding should be undertaken.

19-7. Leverage is always disadvantageous to a firm if the rate of return on
assets is less than _____.

Solution:

The cost of debt.

19-8. The orderly retirement of a bond issue can be facilitated by
_____.

Solution:

A sinking fund.

19-9. If market rates of interest have risen above the coupon rate on a publicly
traded bond issue, the firm is likely to fulfill its sinking fund obligations
through _____.

Solution:

Market purchases of its own bonds.

19-10. What is the major advantage to the firm of subordinated debt over preferred stock?

Solution:

The interest on subordinated debt is deductible as an expense for income tax purposes.

19-11. Why should the interest rate on the new debt, rather than the average cost of capital, be used as the discount factor when calculating the net present value of a refunding operation?

Solution:

There is no risk to the savings—their value is known with relatively complete certainty. With a lower risk, a lower capitalization rate should be employed.

19-12. In what way is an income bond like a share of preferred stock?

Solution:

Management is not required to pay interest if it is not earned.

19-13. Which of the following is a reason for using long-term debt?
a. The firm's management expects a substantial price level rise in future (investors don't share this view).
b. Existing debt ratio is low relative to the industry.
c. Common stock price is temporarily depressed relative to bond prices.
d. b and c.
e. a, b, and c.

Solution:

e. All are reasons for using long-term debt.

19-14. The Par Chemical Company is a leading manufacturer of industrial chem-
icals, plastics, and metals. During 1972, the company sought to raise
$100 million to retire short-term obligations of $50 million and to add
working capital for further growth.

The alternatives available to the company were 25 year, 4.35 percent
sinking fund debentures or the sale of common stock at $60 per share.
In both cases a 1 percent underwriting charge will be incurred. Under the
debenture financing, the firm was obligated to provide for the retirement
of $4 million of principal annually, starting in 1977. Relevant balance
sheet and income statement data are listed below. Assume a 50 percent
tax rate.

Which financing alternative should Par Chemical have chosen?

Chemical industry financial ratios

Current ratio (X)	2.6
Sales to total assets (X)	1.3
Sales to inventory (X)	6.1
Average collection period (days)	46
Current debt/total assets (%)	20
Long-term debt/total assets (%)	20
Preferred/total assets (%)	0-5
Net worth/total assets (%)	55-60
Profits to sales (%)	4.3
Profits to total assets (%)	5.7
Profits to net worth (%)	9.7
Expected growth in earnings and dividends (%)	6.34

Par Chemical Company—Balance sheet, June 30, 1972
(in millions of dollars)

Cash	$ 60		Accounts payable	$70
Net receivables	150		Notes payable, 4.5%	80
Inventories	190		Accruals	50
Total current assets		$ 400	Total current liabilities	$ 200
Investments		50	Long-term debt, 4.4%	100
Net property		550	Common stock, par $5	150
			Retained earnings	100
			Capital surplus	450
Total assets		$1,000	Total claims on assets	$1,000

**Par Chemical Company—Consolidated statement of income,
Years Ended June 30, 1970, 1971, and 1972
(in millions of dollars)**

	1970	1971	1972
Sales (net)	$820	$900	$970
Rental and service income	15	20	20
Total income	835	920	990
Cost of products sold	610	685	720
Depreciation	90	95	100
Selling, administrative, and other expenses	15	20	20
Total expenses	715	800	840
Net operating income (average 18% of sales)	120	120	150
Interest	10	10	8
Income taxes	45	50	62
Net profit for period	$ 65	$ 60	$ 80
Earnings per share of common	2.17	2.00	2.70
Cash dividends per common share	1.40	1.50	1.60
Price range for common stock: high	84	71	70
low	69	40	54

Solution:

a.   Relative costs:

Price-earnings ratio $\dfrac{\$60}{\$2.70}$ = 22 times

Earnings yield $\dfrac{\$2.70}{\$60}$ = 4.5%

Dividend yield $\dfrac{\$1.60}{\$60}$ = 2.66%

Estimated cost of retained earnings $\quad k = \dfrac{D}{P} + g$

$\qquad\qquad\qquad\qquad\qquad = 2.66\% + 6.34\%$

$\qquad\qquad\qquad\qquad\qquad = 9\%$

Debt cost: before tax $\quad = 4.35\%$

after tax $\quad = 2.17\%$

The company's earnings and dividend yield are quite low, and common stock could be sold on a favorable basis. The debt cost (2.17 percent) is also low.

b. Financial structure:

	Industry average	Par Chemical percentage of total assets		
		Now	Debt	Equity
Current debt	20	20	14	14
Long-term debt	20	10	19	9
Total debt	40	30	33	23
Net worth	60	70	67	77

Compared with the indicated industry composite financial structure, Par is relatively heavy in net worth and low in the use of debt. (Admittedly, the dispersion of leverage ratios found in the chemical industry makes its composite a less meaningful guide than those of industries in which leverage ratios are similar among most of the firms in the industry.) In the *pro forma* analysis, it is clear that to raise the funds by common stock would increase the net worth ratio far above the industry average.

On the other hand, the debt issue would bring the ratios closer to the industry average. The total debt figure (33 percent) would still be below the average, and the further leveraging opportunity would continue to exist. This analysis strongly favors the debt alternative.

c. Control:

Currently outstanding shares   30.00 million

New shares $\dfrac{\$100,000,000}{\$60}$ 1.67 million

Total shares   31.67 million

% increase $= \dfrac{1.67}{30} = 5.6\%$

There would be an increase of only 5.6 percent in shares outstanding, of which the added 1.67 million shares would be widely distributed, so there is no danger of loss of control. Generally, control is not an issue in the case of large, listed corporations.

d. Sinking fund: The $4 million sinking fund requirement, plus the additional interest cost of $4.35 million, less an implicit short-term debt cost reduction of $2.25 million ($50 million × 4.5 percent), would give an added fixed cash outlay of $2.35 million until 1977, for the use of debt, and $6.35 million after 1977.

If the net operating income (earnings before interest and taxes) in 1972 were compared with the anticipated new, plus the old, fixed cash outlays, the result would be a 14-times coverage until 1977 and more than a 10-times coverage (150/14.35) for operations after 1977. Earnings have been growing over the past few years, and there is little reason to believe that this trend will cease. Therefore, the added fixed cost burden presents no problems.

e. Break-even chart for Par Chemical's financing alternatives appears on page 190.

The difference between the two alternatives, in terms of the resulting net income, is the interest cost on debt and the number of shares outstanding. Prior to the financing, the total interest cost was $8 million. Under the new debt issue, the interest cost rises to $10.1 million. These figures are explained as follows:

Before financing			After-debt financing		
	Amount	*Cost*		*Amount*	*Cost*
	($ millions)			*($ millions)*	
Notes payable (4.5%)	$ 80	$3.6	Notes payable	$ 30	$ 1.35
Long-term debt			Long-term debt	200	8.75
(4.4%)	100	4.4	(4.4% on $100)		
			(4.35% on $100)		
Total	$180	$8.0	Total	$230	$10.10

It was indicated that $50 million of the new issue is to be used to retire notes payable, and, therefore, the total new debt increases $50 million. For the common stock issue, the interest cost is reduced to $5.75 million ($8 million − 2.25 million).

The approximate break-even point is at $500 million in sales, after which the debt alternative becomes more advantageous in terms of earnings per share because of the increased leverage.

For the common stock issue alternative, the number of shares outstanding increases by 1.66 million shares.

The net increase in debt is $50 million and represents only about a 5 percent increase in the assets of the company. Thus, the break-even analysis of the use of debt versus equity financing indicates an advantage to debt on sales above $500 million, but the advantage in terms of earnings per share is relatively small. Furthermore, the effect on the capitalization rate applicable to common stock earnings is also likely to be slight.

f. The conclusion is that relative costs favor debt, but only slightly. Cash flow analysis favors the sale of common stock. The financial structure pattern favors the use of debt. Par actually sold debt, according to its prospectus dated September 24, 1972.

Use of debt

	$ 0	$ 200	$ 500	$ 600	$ 700	$ 800	$ 900	$1,000	$1,100	$1,200
Sales (millions)	$ 0	$ 200	$ 500	$ 600	$ 700	$ 800	$ 900	$1,000	$1,100	$1,200
Net income before taxes (18%)	0	$36.0	$90.0	$108.0	$126.0	$144.0	$162.0	$180.0	$198.0	$216.0
Interest on debt	10.1	10.1	10.1	10.1	10.1	10.1	10.1	10.1	10.1	10.1
Income subject to tax	—	25.9	79.9	97.9	115.9	133.9	151.9	169.9	187.9	205.9
Tax (50%)	—	12.9	39.9	48.9	57.9	66.9	75.9	84.9	93.9	102.9
Net income after tax	$(10.1)	$13.0	$39.9	$49.0	$58.0	$67.0	$76.0	$85.0	$94.0	$103.0
Earnings per share (30 million shares)	$(0.34)	$ 0.43	$ 1.33	$ 1.63	$ 1.93	$ 2.23	$ 2.53	$ 2.83	$ 3.13	$ 3.43

Use of stock

	$ 0	$ 200	$ 500	$ 600	$ 700	$ 800	$ 900	$1,000	$1,100	$1,200
Sales (millions)	$ 0	$ 200	$ 500	$ 600	$ 700	$ 800	$ 900	$1,000	$1,100	$1,200
Net income before taxes (18%)	$ 0	$ 36	$ 90	$108	$126	$144	$162	$180	$198	$216
Interest on debt	5.8	5.8	5.8	5.8	5.8	5.8	5.8	5.8	5.8	5.8
Income subject to tax*	0	30	84	102	120	138	156	174	192	210
Tax (50%)	0	15	42	51	60	69	78	87	96	105
Net income after tax	$ (5.8)	$ 15	$ 42	$ 51	$ 60	$ 69	$ 78	$ 87	$ 96	$105
Earnings per share (31.66 million shares)	$ (0.18)	$ 0.47	$ 1.33	$ 1.61	$ 1.89	$ 2.17	$ 2.46	$ 2.75	$ 3.04	$ 3.33

* Rounded

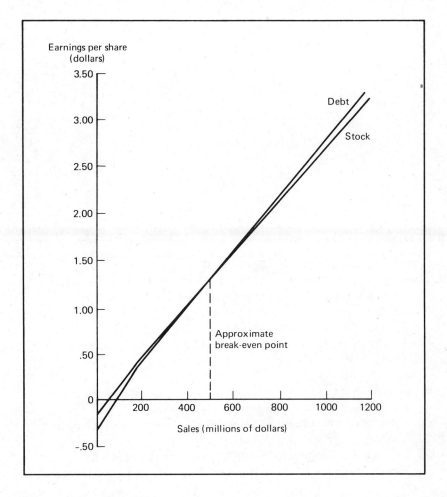

Chapter 20

Warrants and Convertibles

Theme: The sale of debt or preferred stock with convertibility provisions or with warrants can be made at lower interest costs and can provide for a future broadening of the equity base.

I. *Warrants* are long-term options to buy a stated number of shares of common stock during a specified duration at a stated price.

  A. Customary provisions include the following:

    1. The exercise price at which stock may be bought.

    2. A statement of the period during which options can be exercised.

    3. An antidilution clause to protect the warrant in the event of a stock dividend or stock split.

  B. The market value of warrants increases as these factors increase:

    1. The duration of the option period.

    2. The market value of common stock relative to the stated purchase price (the exercise price).

    3. The number of common shares to be purchased by each warrant.

    4. The speculative possibilities—that is, the growth potential—of the common stock.

II. Determinants of the value of warrants.

  A. Theoretical market value of warrants:

$$
\begin{array}{cccc}
\text{Theoretical} & \text{Market price} & \text{Option} & \text{Number of shares each} \\
\text{value of} \quad = & \text{of} \quad - & \text{purchase} \quad \times & \text{warrant entitles owner} \\
\text{warrant} & \text{common stock} & \text{price} & \text{to purchase}
\end{array}
$$

  B. Actual price of a warrant.

    1. Warrant usually sells above theoretical value.

    2. Premium over theoretical value is largest when price of common is at a low unit level.

    3. The amount of the premium decreases as the price of the common rises.

    4. Above some absolute level of common stock price, the premium becomes constant.

C. Reasons why the size of the premium diminishes as the price of the common stock rises.
1. Declining leverage impact.
2. Increasing magnitude of potential losses.

III. Reasons for using warrants include the following:
A. Warrants are usually used by growing firms to reduce the interest cost on debt and to avoid restrictive indenture provisions.
B. Warrants tend to widen the market for the firm's debt.
C. Warrants can provide for additional equity funds in the future.

IV. Appraisal of the use of warrants.
A. Advantages:
1. Warrants allow a balanced financing of debt and equity.
2. They aid the sale of debt and reduce interest rates on debt.
3. They can result in the future sale of equities at prices higher than the current market value.
B. Disadvantages:
1. The long-term call on the common stock is a form of dilution.
2. Exercise of the warrants increases the equity base and, therefore, reduces the effects of trading on the equity.
3. Warrants can be exercised and bring in funds at a time when the firm has no need for additional capital.

V. Convertible securities are bonds or preferred stock which are exchangeable for common stock at the holder's option. Typical terms of the conversion privilege include:
A. The *conversion ratio*—the number of shares of common for which the convertible may be exchanged.
B. The *conversion price*—the effective price paid per share of common upon conversion.
1. Conversion price $= \dfrac{\text{par value of convertible security}}{\text{number of shares received on conversion}}$
2. Usually the conversion premium is 10 to 20 percent above market price at the time the convertible is issued; that is, the conversion price exceeds the market price of the stock by 10 to 20 percent.
C. Some convertibles have decreasing conversion ratios (increasing conversion prices) over time.
D. Convertibles also include a clause protecting the holder against dilution due to stock splits or stock dividends.

VI. Use of convertibles.
A. Convertibles provide a hedge against uncertainty.
1. In depression, they afford the protection of senior debt.
2. In boom or inflation, both the price of the convertible and the value of the conversion privilege increase.
B. Interest rates on convertible bonds are always lower than those on non-

convertible bonds of equivalent risk; investors who buy convertibles give up income for the hope of capital gain.

C. There has been a pronounced increase in the use of convertibles in recent years; financial managers seem to be using convertibles more to facilitate the raising of future equity capital rather than as a sweetener to reduce the interest cost of debt issues.

VII. Advantages to the use of convertibles include:

A. Convertibles permit the sale of debt at low interest rates.

B. Convertibles provide a method of selling equity at prices higher than the current market prices.

C. The call provision gives the company a means of forcing conversion whenever the market price of the stock exceeds the conversion price.

D. Convertibles provide low-cost capital during a period when earnings on assets are being developed.

VIII. Disadvantages of convertibles include the following:

A. A delay in financing could possibly enable the sale of an equity issue at prices higher than those obtained through a convertible issue.

B. The market price of the common might not rise above the conversion price. Thus, a high debt-equity ratio would remain.

IX. Warrants and convertibles perform the same basic functions, but differences should be noted.

A. The exercise of convertibles does not ordinarily bring additional funds to the company. The exercise of warrants does bring in additional funds.

B. Conversion results in reduced debt ratios. The exercise of warrants strengthens the equity position, but debt (or preferred) remains outstanding.

C. Because of the call feature, convertibles give the firm greater control over the timing of capital structure changes than do warrants.

PROBLEMS

20-1. XYZ Corporation's warrants are currently selling at an $8 premium over the theoretical value. Each warrant entitles its owner to purchase two shares of common stock for $50 (or $25 per share). If the common stock is presently selling for $45, what is the market price of the warrant?

Solution:

Step 1. Use the formula:

$$\text{Theoretical value} = \left(\begin{matrix} \text{Market price of} \\ \text{common stock} \end{matrix} - \begin{matrix} \text{Option} \\ \text{price} \end{matrix} \right) \times \begin{matrix} \text{Number of shares each} \\ \text{warrant entitles owner} \\ \text{to purchase} \end{matrix}$$

$$= (\$45 - \$25) \times 2$$
$$= \$40, \text{ theoretical value of warrant.}$$

Step 2. Use the formula:

Market price of warrant = Theoretical value of warrant + Premium
$$= \$40 + \$8$$
$$= \$48, \text{ market price of warrant.}$$

20-2. The call price on ABC's $1,000 par value convertible bond is $1,100. Given a conversion price of $25 per share (that is, each bond can be converted into 40 shares of stock), which of the choices below is the lowest price at which the stock can sell for and still have bondholders convert rather than submit their bonds for redemption in the event of a call?

a. $30.01　　　　　　d. $25.01
b. $28.51　　　　　　e. $20.51
c. $27.50

Solution:

c. $\dfrac{\$1100, \text{ call price}}{40, \text{ conversion ratio}}$ = $27.50, minimum price for conversion.

20-3. In the preceding problem, what would you expect the conversion ratio (shares received on conversion per $1,000 bond) to be after ABC declared a 20 percent stock dividend?

Solution:

0.20 stock dividend × 40 shares = 8 additional shares
40 + 8 = 48 shares, the new conversion ratio

20-4. At time of issue, what price relationship generally exists between the subscription price on warrants and rights, and common stock?

Solution: The subscription price of warrants is generally above the market price of the stock; that of rights is set below the stock price.

20-5. True or false: Warrants generally sell above their theoretical value.

Solution: True. This is always true unless arbitrageurs fail to fulfill their function.

20-6. Where is the conversion price on a convertible bond generally set?

Solution: Above the price of the stock.

20-7. True or false. The coupon rate on a convertible bond is usually higher than on an equivalent straight bond.

Solution: False. It is typically lower because of the advantage to the investor of the conversion privilege.

20-8. In which of the following cases would current financing by means of debt with warrants be inappropriate?
   a. External funds needed now but no additional requirement expected for many years.
   b. External funds needed now with a continuing requirement for additional funds.
   c. A large amount of external funds needed now with diminishing requirements expected for next several years.
   d. Some external funds needed now with an expected increase in funds required for next several years.

Solution: a.

20-9. The Mark Jackson Tube Company's capital consists of 9,000 shares of common stock and 3,000 warrants. Each warrant is capable of buying four shares of common at $75 per share. The warrants are protected against dilution (that is, the subscription price is adjusted downward in the event of a stock dividend or a stock split). The company also issues rights to buy one new share of common stock at $55 for every three shares held. With the stock selling with rights at $95, compute:
   a. The theoretical value of the rights before stock sells ex-rights.
   b. The new subscription price of the warrant after the rights issue.

Solution:

a. Value of one right $= \dfrac{Mo - S}{N + 1} = \dfrac{\$95 - \$55}{3 + 1} = \dfrac{\$40}{4} = \$10$

b. Value of the warrant (before rights offering) = (market price of common stock less option price) $\times$ number of shares each warrant entitles owner to purchase = ($95 − $75) $\times$ 4 = $80

In order to protect warrant holders against the dilution effect of the rights issue, the theoretical value of the warrants must remain the same after the stock goes ex-rights. Therefore: with the market price of stock ex-rights = $95 − $10 = $85 and the value of the warrant held at $80

$$\$80 = (85 - x)4$$
$$x = \$65, \text{ new subscription price}$$

20-10. Bernard Paint, Inc., has the following balance sheet:

Balance Sheet 1

Current assets	$120,000	Current debt	$ 50,000
Net fixed assets	130,000	Common stock, par value $2	60,000
		Earned surplus	140,000
Total assets	$250,000	Total claims	$250,000

The firm earns 20 percent on total assets before taxes (assume a 50 percent tax rate).

In the following few years, sales are expected to double and the financing needs of the firm will double. The firm decides to sell debentures to meet these needs. It is undecided, however, whether to sell convertible debentures or debentures with warrants. The new balance sheet would appear as follows:

Balance Sheet 2

Current assets	$220,000	Current debt	$ 90,000
Net fixed assets	230,000	Debentures	170,000
		Common stock, par value $2	60,000
		Earned surplus	180,000
Total assets	$500,000	Total claims	$500,000

The convertible debentures would pay 7 percent interest and would be convertible into 20 shares of common stock for each $1,000 debenture. The debentures with warrants would carry an 8 percent coupon and entitle each holder of a $1,000 debenture to buy ten shares of common stock at $70. John Bernard owns 80 percent of the company before the financing.

a. Assume that convertible debentures are sold and all are later converted. Show the new balance sheet, disregarding any changes in retained earnings.

b. Complete the firm's income statement after the debentures have all been converted.

c. Now, instead of convertibles, assume that debentures with warrants were issued. Assume further that the warrants were all exercised. Show the new balance sheet figures.

d. Complete the firm's income statement after the debenture warrants have all been exercised.

Solution:

a. 20 (shares) × 170 (debentures) = 3,400 (new shares) × $2 (par value) = $6,800 (addition to common stock account at par value)

$170,000 − $6,800 = $163,200, paid in surplus

Balance Sheet 3

		Current debt	$ 90,000
		Debentures	—
		Common stock, par $2	66,800
		Paid in surplus	163,200
		Earned surplus	180,000
Total assets	$500,000	Total claims on assets	$500,000

b. Net income after all charges except debenture interest and before taxes,

(20 percent of total assets),	$100,000
Debenture interest,	0
Taxable income	$100,000
Federal income tax, 50%	50,000
Net income after taxes,	$ 50,000
Earnings per share after taxes,	$1.50	($50,000/33,400 = $1.50)

c. 10 (shares) × 170 (debentures) = 1,700 (new shares) × $2 (par value) = $3,400 (addition to common stock account at par value)
$70 (option price) × 1,700 (shares) = $119,000
$119,000 − $3,400 = $115,600, (paid in surplus)

Balance Sheet 4

		Current debt	$ 90,000
		Debentures	170,000
		Common stock, par $2	63,400
		Paid-in surplus	115,600
		Earned surplus	180,000
Total assets	$619,000	Total claims on assets	$619,000

d. Net income after all charges except debenture interest and before taxes.

$619,000 × 0.20 =	$123,800
Debenture interest,	13,600
Taxable income	$110,200
Federal income tax,	55,100
Net income after taxes,	$ 55,100
Earnings per share after taxes,	$1.74	($55,100/31,700 = $1.74)

Part VII

Valuation in Mergers and Corporate Readjustment

Chapter 21

External Growth: Mergers and Holding Companies

Theme: Mergers and holding company formations have played important roles in the growth of firms. Since financial managers are required to participate in appraising the desirability of a prospective merger and in the evaluation of companies involved in the merger, these materials are a necessary part of their background.

I. Definitions:

  A. *Merger*—When firm A acquires firm B and firm B entirely disappears.

  B. *Combination* or *consolidation*—When firms A and B join to form firm C.

  C. *Purchase*—An accounting term indicating acquisition by large company of small company and complete absorption of small company.

  D. *Pooling*—An accounting term indicating a combination of companies of about equal size in which the once separate managements and firms continue to carry on important functions.

  E. In general usage, "merger" means any combination that forms one economic unit from two or more previous ones.

II. Reasons for seeking growth:

  A. Research—Certain types of research can be performed best by large firms.

  B. Top management skills—Skilled executives are an extremely scarce commodity, and it is often economical to spread their talents over a relatively large enterprise.

  C. Operating economies—For some types of production, the average cost per unit of output is lower when large-scale plants and distribution systems are used.

  D. Risk reduction—Risk is reduced by diversification in large enterprises. Tax considerations add to the importance of this factor.

  E. Market capitalization rates—Market capitalization rates are lower for larger firms, giving them a lower cost of capital.

III. Advantages of use of mergers versus internal growth:

  A. Speed—New facilities acquired more quickly.

  B. Cost—Purchase of existing facilities may cost less.

1. Securities of a desired firm may be selling for less than cost of building similar facilities outright.
2. May obtain desired personnel through merger where direct hiring might have failed.
C. Financing—Sometimes acquisitions can be financed when it is not possible to finance internal growth.
D. Risk—New product, process, organization, and so on, may be developed with less uncertainty.
   1. In the acquisition of a going concern, the revenue-yielding ability of facilities may have already been demonstrated.
   2. New process or new product acquired may have also demonstrated revenue capability.
E. Mergers may be the best method of obtaining stability at certain stages of industrial growth.
F. Taxes and their effect on mergers.
   1. High level of taxes since World War II had effect of increasing merger movement.
   2. A study showed that in one-fourth of all assets sold and one-third of all assets acquired since World War II, taxes were an important consideration.
   3. Any tax loss from a merger can be offset against assured income to reduce taxes.
G. Competitive advantages to merger.
   1. Acquisition of a company already in a desired market may cut down cost of entrance and of battling competition to get a foothold.
   2. Merger may bring about market control.
      a. Such actions may bring federal intervention.
      b. Manager must therefore consider effects as well as his own motives in a proposed merger.
IV. Arriving at the terms of a merger.
   A. Quantitative factors to be considered on the basis of their trends and variability.
      1. *Present earnings* and *expected future earnings* after the merger, which are reflected in expectations about the effects of the merger on the surviving firm's *growth rate*, are perhaps the most important determinants of the price that will be paid for a firm that is being acquired.
      2. *Dividends* paid are likely to have little influence on the market price of companies with a record of high growth and profitability.
      3. *Market prices* clearly influence the price that must be paid in an acquisition, but the acquisition price is likely to exceed the current market price because:
         a. A low current market price may be reflective of industry-wide conditions rather than of the true value of the firm.

b. The acquired company may be worth more to an informed purchaser than it is in the general market.

c. Higher prices will be offered to current stockholders as an inducement to sell.

4. *Book value.* Depending on whether or not asset values are indicative of the approximate value of the merged firm, book values may exert an important influence on the terms of the merger.

5. *Net current assets.* Net current assets are an indication of the amount of liquidity being purchased; this can be an important factor in the merger.

a. Acquiring a company with high net current assets may leave the acquiring company in a position for further mergers.

b. If it is debt free, the acquired firm's assets and earning power may be used as security for the purchase loan.

B. Qualitative factors to be considered are:

1. Management experience.

2. Quality of the engineering staff.

3. Abilities of the sales organization.

4. Possible economies through cost saving.

5. Degree to which one firm complements the operations of the other.

6. Synergistic, or 2 + 2 = 5, effects represent reinforcement of capabilities in a very broad sense.

V. Effects of mergers on earnings per share.

A. Illustrative examples

1. Assume the following facts for two companies:

	Company A	Company B
Total earnings	$20,000	$50,000
Number of shares of common stock	5,000	10,000
Earnings per share of stock	$ 4.00	$ 5.00
Price-earnings ratio per share	15X	12X
Market price per share	$ 60.00	$ 60.00

2. The firms agree to merge, with B, the surviving firm, acquiring the shares of A by a one-for-one exchange of stock.

3. Assuming no immediate increase in earnings, the effects on earnings per share are shown in the following tabulation:

	Shares of Company B owned after merger	Earnings per share	
		Before merger	After merger
A's stockholders	5,000	$4	$4.67
B's stockholders	10,000	5	4.67
Total	15,000		

4. Earnings will *increase* by 67 cents for A's stockholders, but they will *decline* by 33 cents for B's.
5. The effects on market value are less certain: Will A's or B's P/E ratio prevail after the merger?
6. If the merger takes place on the basis of earnings, neither earnings dilution nor earnings appreciation will take place.

	Shares of Company B owned after merger	Earnings per old share	
		Before merger	After merger
A shareholders	4,000	$4	$4
B shareholders	10,000	5	5
Total	14,000		

B. Generalizations on initial effects on earnings per share.
1. If terms of merger reflect current market prices and price-earnings ratios are equal, neither earnings dilution nor earnings accretion will result.
2. If exchange terms are based on market prices and the prevailing price-earnings ratios differ, initial earnings accretion and dilution will result.
3. Any initial earnings dilution or accretion may be offset by resulting growth rates of the company as compared with what the growth rates of the individual companies would have been.
4. If synergy is present in a merger, future earnings per share for stockholders of both companies may be greater than earnings per share would have been for the companies without the merger.
VI. Accounting policies in mergers—Guidelines of the APB of the AICPA, in APB 16 and APB 17, effective October 31, 1970.
A. Pooling of interests.
1. Six conditions—if met, pooling of interest *must* be used.
a. Acquired firm's stockholders continue ownership.
b. Basis for accounting for the assets of acquired entity is unchanged.
c. Each entity had been autonomous; no more than 10% common ownership before the merger.
d. Single transactions; contingent payouts not permitted in poolings, but may be used in purchases.
e. Payment by acquiring company in common stock for substantially all of the voting common stock of company acquired; substantially defined at 90%.
f. No intention to dispose of a significant portion of the assets within two years after the merger.
2. Accounting treatment.
a. The total assets of the surviving firm are equal to the sum of the assets of the two independent companies.
b. No good will is involved.

    c. The excess of market value paid over book value is charged first against capital surplus and then against retained earnings.

B. Purchase

  1. Involves

    a. New owners.

    b. New basis for accounting for assets of the acquired entity.

    c. Possibility of consideration paid not equal to book value of entity acquired.

  2. Accounting treatment.

    a. The excess of market value over book value acquired is set up as goodwill and written off over some period.

    b. Total assets after the purchase may therefore exceed the sum of the total assets of the individual companies.

  3. Treatment of intangibles

    a. When payment is greater than acquired net worth, to extent appropriate the excess is associated with tangible depreciable assets. Provides tax deductions.

    b. Any excess not so assigned gives rise to goodwill account.

    c. Goodwill is depreciable, but not tax deductible.

    d. Goodwill must be written off over some reasonable period no longer than 40 years in length (write off of 2.5% per year).

VII. A holding company is formed for the purpose of owning the stock of other companies, which operate as separate legal entities.

A. Advantages of holding companies:

  1. In general, advantages of the holding company may include any which accrue to large scale operations.

  2. Advantages specific to the holding company form include these:

    a. Control with fractional ownership is possible with widely distributed stock.

      1. A firm in a secular decline may use funds to buy a position in a growth industry.

      2. Greater leverage is obtainable through fractional ownership.

    b. Isolation of risks—Each firm in a holding company is a separate legal identity, and the obligations of any one unit are separate from the obligations of the other units.

    c. Approval not required—Stockholder approval is required before a merger can take place. This is not necessary if a holding company purchases the securities of another firm.

B. Disadvantages of holding companies include:

  1. *Partial multiple taxation*—If the holding company does not own 80 percent of the subsidiary's stock and does not file consolidated tax returns, it is subjected to taxes on dividends received from the subsidiary.

  2. *Risks from excessive pyramiding*—The leverage effects possible in holding companies can subject the holding company to the risks of high leverage. Leverage in holding companies represents a magnification of trading on the equity with both the potential benefits and potential losses.

3. *Ease of dissolution*—The Antitrust Division of the Department of Justice can much more easily force the breakup of a holding company than it can the dissolution of two completely merged firms.

VIII. Tender offers.

  A. Definition.

    1. A group seeking a controlling interest in another corporation invites the stockholders of the firm it is seeking to control to submit, or tender, their shares in exchange at a specified price.

    2. A tender is a direct appeal to stockholders, so it is not necessary to receive approval of the management of the acquired firm.

  B. Advantages.

    1. No prior approval is required.

    2. The percentage of shares to be acquired can be specified in advance.

  C. Disadvantages.

    1. Conflict and dissension between firms that are joined.

    2. Legislative controls enacted July 29, 1968:

      a. The acquiring firm must give 30 days' notice both to management of the acquired firm and to the Securities and Exchange Commission.

      b. When substantial blocks of stocks are purchased through tender offers, the beneficial owner must be disclosed as well as the party providing the funds.

PROBLEMS

21-1. Companies A and B have the following financial data:

	Company A	*Company B*
Total earnings	$50,000	$80,000
Number of shares of stock outstanding	15,000	20,000
Earnings per share of stock	$ 3.33	$ 4.00
Price-earnings ratio per share	12X	9X
Market price per share	$39.93	$36.00

  a. *A* and *B* have agreed to merge. *B*, the surviving firm, is to acquire the shares of *A* by a one-for-one exchange of stock. Assuming no increase in total earnings, what will be the effect on EPS for *B*'s stockholders?

  Solution:

    1. $ 80,000
       50,000
      $130,000, total earnings of *A* and *B*

    2. $\dfrac{\$130,000}{35,000 \text{ shares}}$ = $3.71, EPS after merger

3. $4.00
    3.71
$0.29, decline

b. If the merger of A and B is based on earnings per share instead of relative market prices, what will be the change in earnings after the merger for a holder of 100 shares of company A stock?

Solution: No change.

$$\frac{EPS\ A}{EPS\ B} = \frac{\$3.33}{\$4.00} = 0.8325, \text{number of shares of } B$$
$$\text{for each share of } A$$

100
X 0.8325
    83.25, shares of B after merger

83.25
X $4
$333.00, total earnings after merger

100
X $3.33
$333.00, total earnings before merger; therefore, no change.

c. What is the new expected growth rate of the merged firm if prior to the merger, A is expected to grow at 10 percent and B at 6 percent? Assume no synergistic effects occur in the merger.

Solution:

	Company A	Company B	A + B
Total earnings:	$50,000	$80,000	$130,000

$$\text{Expected growth rate } g = \frac{\$\ 50,000}{\$130,000} \times 0.10 + \frac{\$\ 80,000}{\$130,000} \times 0.06 = 0.0754 = 7.54\%$$

d. Which of the following is *not* typically considered a disadvantage in a holding company situation?
    1. Pyramiding.
    2. Partial multiple taxation.
    3. Risk reduction from diversification.
    4. Legal vulnerability.
    5. None of above.

Solution: 3.

e. Circle the criteria that suggests using a purchase rather than a pooling of interest for two firms that are about to merge.
  1. Small/large size differential between the firms.
  2. Ownership interest of the acquired firm is/is not substantially reduced.
  3. The purchased assets of the acquired company are/are not sold off.
  4. The management of the acquired company is/is not retained.

Solution:

  1. large.
  2. is.
  3. are.
  4. is not.

21-2. Given the following balance sheets:

The Horning Company–Consolidated balance sheet
(in thousands of dollars)

Cash	$ 700	Borrowings	$ 500
Other current assets	300	Common stock	1,100
Net property	1,000	Surplus	400
Total assets	$2,000	Total claims on assets	$2,000

A Company–Balance sheet

Current assets	$250	Net worth	$ $500
Net property	250		
Total assets	$500	Total net worth	$500

a. The Horning Company buys operating Company *A* with "free" cash of $500. Show the new consolidated balance sheet for Horning after the acquisition.

Solution:

The Horning Company–Consolidated balance sheet
(in thousands of dollars)

Cash	$ 200	Borrowings	$ 500
Other current assets	550	Common stock	1,100
Net property	1,250	Surplus	400
Total assets	$2,000	Total claims	$2,000

b. Instead of buying *A*, the Horning Company now buys operating Company *B* with "free" cash of $700. The balance sheet of *B* Company follows.

B Company–Balance sheet

Current assets	$ 300	Borrowings	$ 300
Net property	700	Net worth	700
Total assets	$1,000	Total claims on assets	$1,000

Show the new consolidated balance sheet for Horning after the acquisition.

Solution:

The Horning Company–Consolidated balance sheet
(in thousands of dollars)

Cash	$ 0	Borrowings	$ 800
Other current assets	600	Common stock	1,100
Net property	1,700	Surplus	400
Total assets	$2,300	Total claims on assets	$2,300

c. What are the implications of your consolidated balance sheets for measuring the growth of firms resulting from acquisitions?

Solution:

When the acquisition is by cash and no debt is assumed, as in Part I, the total consolidated cash assets of Horning are not increased by the acquisition. To measure growth, the composition of Horning's assets before and after the acquisition must be analyzed.

When the acquisition is by cash and debt is taken over as in Part II, the total consolidated assets of Horning increase only by the amount of debt taken over, not by the full amount of assets acquired. The composition of Horning's assets would again have to be studied.

Of course, the best measure of the extent of acquisition by a firm is the dollar amount of sales of the firm acquired. The volume of sales is a better measure of the impact of a firm on the market than are the total assets since sales to total asset ratios vary according to the line of business.

21-3. Rixy is a holding company owning the entire common stock of Minor Company and Operating Company. The balance sheet as of December 31, 1972 for each subsidiary is identical with the following one.

**Balance sheet,
December 31, 1972**

Current assets	$2,400,000	Current liabilities	$ 600,000
Fixed assets, net	3,600,000	First mortgage bonds	
		(4%)	2,000,000
		Preferred stock (5%)	1,000,000
		Common stock (par $10)	2,000,000
		Surplus	400,000
Total assets	$6,000,000	Total claims	$6,000,000

Each company earns $660,000 annually before taxes and before interest and preferred dividends. A 50 percent tax rate is assumed.

a. What is the annual rate of return on each company's net worth (common stock plus surplus)?

Solution:

$660,000, income
  80,000, interest on bonds
$580,000, income before taxes
 290,000, income tax
$290,000, income after taxes
  50,000, preferred stock dividends
$240,000, earnings available to common

$$\frac{\$240,000 \text{ earnings}}{\$2,400,000, \text{ net worth}} = 10\%$$

b. Construct a balance sheet for Rixy based on the following assumptions: (1) The only asset of the holding company is the common stock of the two subsidiaries; this stock is carried at par (not book). (2) The holding company has $500,000 of 4 percent coupon debt and $1,000,000 of 6 percent preferred stock.

Solution:

Balance sheet of Rixy

		Debt (4%)	$ 500,000
		Preferred (6%)	1,000,000
		Common stock (par $10)	2,500,000
Total assets			
($2,000,000 × 2)	$4,000,000	Total claims	$4,000,000

c. What is the rate of return on the book value of the holding company's common stock?

Solution: Since each company earns $240,000 annually after taxes and other deductions, total gross receipts are $480,000 or (2 × $240,000).

Book value = common stock + surplus = $2,500,000 + 0 = $2,500,000

Interest costs are:
    Debt at 4% of $500,000 = $20,000

Preferred costs are:
    Preferred at 6% of $1,000,000 = $60,000
    $480,000, income
    $\underline{-20,000}$, interest on debt
    460,000, income after interest
    $\underline{-60,000}$, preferred stock dividends
    $400,000, earnings available to common

Rate of return on book value of Rixy = $\dfrac{\$400,000}{\$2,500,000}$ = 16.0%

Note that no income tax is deducted here since the Rixy Company owns 100 percent of its subsidiaries' stock and therefore may deduct all of this income from taxable income.

d. How could the rate of return in part c be increased?

Solution: More leverage by the subsidiaries and/or the holding company could increase the rate of return.

e. What investment is necessary to control the three companies under the assumptions of the initial conditions?

Solution: It depends on how widely the holding company's stock is held. For example, a small percentage of the stock in General Motors would permit control. On the other hand, a far greater percentage of Ford stock would be necessary to gain control.

f. If ownership of 30 percent of the holding companies' common stock ($2.5 million of common) could control all three firms, what percentage would this be of the total assets?

Solution:

30% of $2.5 million = $750,000
Total assets controlled = 2 × total operating assets of each subsidiary
            = 2 × $6,000,000 = $12,000,000

$\dfrac{\$75,000}{\$12,000,000}$ = 6.25% of total operating assets
            will control all three firms

21-4. You are given the following data on two companies:

Terms of merger analysis

	Company A	Company B	Adjustments or ratio	Consolidated statement
Current assets	$120,000	$120,000		1. _____
Fixed assets	80,000	80,000		2. _____
Total assets	$200,000	$200,000		3. _____
Current liabilities	$ 60,000	$ 60,000		4. _____
Long-term debt	40,000	40,000		5. _____
Total debt,* 5%	$100,000	$100,000		6. _____
Common stock, par value $5	$ 50,000	$ 50,000	1. _____	7. _____
Capital surplus	40,000	40,000	2. _____	8. _____
Earned surplus	10,000	10,000		9. _____
Total claims on assets	$200,000	$200,000		10. _____
			Ratios	
1. Number of shares of stock	10,000	10,000		1. _____
2. Book value per share	_____	_____	1. _____	2. _____
3. Amount of profit before interest and taxes†	$ 45,000	$ 35,000		3. _____
4. Earnings per share	_____	_____	2. _____	4. _____
5. Price/earnings ratio	30	20		
6. Market price of stock	_____	_____	3. _____	
7. Working capital per share	_____	_____	4. _____	
8. Dividends per share, 50% payout	_____	_____	5. _____	
9. Exchange ratio	_____	_____	6. _____	(A/B)
10. Equivalent earnings per old share	_____	_____		

*Average rate on interest-bearing and noninterest-bearing debt combined.
†Assume a 50% tax rate.

Use the market price of stock relation as the basis for the terms of exchange of stock in the old company for stock in the new company (2 shares of *AB* for 1 share of *A*, or 1 share of *AB* for 1 share of *B*). Then complete all calculations for filling in all the blank spaces, including the adjustments for making the consolidated statement. Treat this problem as a situation that the SEC and accountants would refer to as a pooling of interests.

Solution:

Terms of merger analysis

	Company A	Company B	Adjustments or ratio	Consolidated statement
Current assets	$120,000	$120,000		1. $240,000
Fixed assets	80,000	80,000		2. 160,000
Total assets	$200,000	$200,000		3. $400,000
Current liabilities	$ 60,000	$ 60,000		4. $120,000
Long-term debt	40,000	40,000		5. 80,000
Total debt* 5%	$100,000	$100,000		6. $200,000
Common stock, par value $5	$ 50,000	$ 50,000	1. Dr. $50,000‡	7. $150,000
Capital surplus	40,000	40,000	2. Cr. 50,000‡	8. 30,000
Earned surplus	10,000	10,000		9. 20,000
Total claims on assets	$200,000	$200,000		10. $400,000
			Ratios	
1. Number of shares of stock	10,000	10,000		1. 30,000
2. Book value per share	$10.00	$10.00	1.0	2. $6.67
3. Amount of profit before interest and taxes†	$ 45,000	$ 35,000		3. $ 80,000
4. Earnings per share	$ 2.00	$ 1.50	4/3	4. $1.17**
5. Price-earnings ratio	30	20		
6. Market price of stock per share	$60.00	$30.00	2.0	
7. Working capital per share	$ 6.00	$ 6.00	1.0	
8. Dividends per share, 50% payout	$ 1.00	$ 0.75	4/3	
9. Exchange ratio	2/1	1/1	2/1	
10. Equivalent earning per share	$ 2.33	$ 1.17		

*Average rate on interest-bearing and noninterest-bearing debt combined.   5,000 + 5,000
†Assumes a 50% tax rate.

$$**\text{New } EPS = \frac{(\text{Earnings} - \text{Interest}) \times (1 - \text{Tax rate})}{\text{Number of shares outstanding}} = \frac{(\$80,000 - \$10,000) \times (1 - 0.50)}{30,000}$$

$$= \$1.17$$

‡The point in these adjustments is as follows: There are 30,000 shares outstanding after the merger. 30,000 × $5 par value = $150,000 = common stock. To force common stock to equal $50,000, take $50,000 from "capital surplus" and add to "common stock."

Chapter 22

Failure, Reorganization,
and Liquidation

Theme: The financial manager has double responsibility in relation to financial difficulties. If it is his own firm that has financial problems, the financial manager's ability may make the difference between loss of ownership of the firm and the rehabilitation of the firm as a going enterprise. When other firms fall into financial difficulties, knowledge of the rights of creditors may make the difference between large losses and small or no losses.

I. Financial life cycle.

   A. The life cycle of an industrial firm can be described in four steps:

      1. Experimentation period.

      2. Rapid growth period.

      3. Maturity.

      4. Decline.

   B. Financial readjustment problems appear most often during the declining phase of the industry life cycle.

II. Failure.

   A. Economic—A firm's revenues do not cover costs.

   B. Financial—Financial failure signifies insolvency.

      1. In equity sense, if a firm cannot meet its current obligations as they come due (even though the total assets may exceed its total liabilities).

      2. In bankruptcy sense, if a firm's total liabilities exceed total assets, the net worth of the firm is negative.

   C. Cause of failure.

      1. Neglect.

      2. Fraud.

      3. Disaster.

      4. Management incompetence.

III. Informal reorganization.

   A. *Quasi reorganization* is a series of accounting adjustments designed to remove an operating deficit.

      1. The adjustments meet commonly accepted accounting practice if:

     a. New asset values are realistic.

     b. Full disclosure of the procedure is made before stockholder approval is sought.

     c. Adjustments reflect the circumstances causing the revaluation.

  2. The operation may enable the payment of dividends out of future earnings. If no reorganization were undertaken, the firm would have to delay dividend payments until earnings offset the deficit in earned surplus.

B. The alternatives available to meet insolvency or bankruptcy include:

  1. *Extension* involves the postponement of the due date of an obligation.

  2. *Composition* is a voluntary reduction of creditor claims. A pro rata cash settlement is paid to the creditors. Advantages of composition are (1) bankruptcy costs are avoided, and (2) debtor avoids stigma of bankruptcy.

  3. *A combination settlement* is a mixture of extension and composition.

  4. Procedure for extensions, compositions, and combination settlements.

     a. An adjustment bureau normally arranges and conducts meetings between the debtor and his creditors.

     b. The creditors are represented by a committee composed of the largest four or five creditors and one or two representatives of the smaller creditors.

     c. The bureau receives the facts of the case and sends investigators to examine the firm.

     d. The bureau and the creditors' committee prepare an adjustment plan.

     e. Meetings are held between the debtor and the creditors' committee to reach a final agreement. An agreement is feasible under the following conditions.

       1. Debtor is a good moral risk.

       2. Debtor has the ability to recover.

       3. General business conditions are favorable.

C. Appraisal of voluntary settlements.

  1. Advantages include its simplicity, minimum costs, and maximum benefits to creditors.

  2. Disadvantages include the fact that control of the business stays with the debtor and the nuisance of small creditors who demand full payment.

IV. Formal reorganization.

A. Formal reorganization may take several forms, all of which have these features in common:

  1. The firm is either insolvent or bankrupt.

  2. New funds are needed for working capital or property improvement.

  3. Management must be improved.

B. A sound reorganization plan meets the tests of fairness and feasibility.

  1. The basic doctrine of *fairness* is met if claims are scaled down in order of their contractual priority and if junior claimants make an additional cash contribution to the firm.

2. A reorganization plan is *feasible* if it will not result in subsequent default. In order to prevent another default it may be necessary to:
   a. Improve management.
   b. Reduce inventories.
   c. Modernize plant and equipment.
   d. Improve operations in the sales and finance areas.
   e. Revamp product policies.
V. *Federal bankruptcy laws* provide a means for insolvent debtors to discharge their obligations and begin new businesses unhampered by prior debt.
   A. Petition for bankruptcy can be initiated voluntarily by the debtor or involuntarily by the creditors.
   B. Bankruptcy case procedure:
      1. In succession, the petition is filed; the debtor is subpoenaed; the court adjudges him bankrupt if there is no contest; a referee is appointed to act in place of the judge.
      2. A receiver may be appointed as property custodian until the creditors appoint a trustee at their first meeting.
      3. The court appoints property appraisers.
      4. The trustee converts the assets to cash. He cannot sell assets at less than 75 percent of appraised value.
      5. Proceeds minus liquidation costs are paid out as dividends.
      6. The trustee makes an accounting to the creditors and the referee.
      7. The U.S. Attorney General examines the case for possibility of fraud, and, if necessary, initiates criminal proceedings.
      8. If no criminal proceedings are initiated, the debtor is discharged of his obligations and may begin business again.
   C. The priority of claims of general creditors is scaled down as follows:
      1. The ratio of available funds to creditors' claims is calculated.
      2. The ratio is applied to the amounts claimed.
      3. Allocations to subordinated creditors are transferred to senior creditors until their claims are satisfied.
      4. The balance, if any, is allocated to the stockholders.
   D. Weaknesses in bankruptcy proceedings.
      1. An involuntary bankruptcy case will be dismissed if the bankrupt proves himself solvent. The creditors must bear the court costs.
      2. Proceedings are cumbersome and costly. In approximately two-thirds of the cases there are no assets to liquidate.
      3. The trustee may be unfamiliar with the business, and, therefore, management of the properties during receivership may be inefficient.
      4. Creditors should be alert to potential fraud through the sale of assets at lower than market value.
      5. Creditors often lack interest in the proceedings and fail to press their claims vigorously.

VI. The priority of claims in bankruptcy.
   A. The order of priority:
     1. Cost of administering the estate.
     2. Wages due workers.
     3. Taxes due.
     4. Secured creditors.
     5. Unsecured creditors.
     6. Preferred stock.
     7. Common stock.

PROBLEMS

22-1. Which of the following are generally considered stages in the life cycle of a firm?
    a. Experimentation.
    b. Exploitation.
    c. Maturity.
    d. Reorganization.
    e. a, b, and c.
    f. All of the above.

Solution: e.

22-2. True or false: You would expect a creditor of an insolvent firm to prefer composition over assignment if he had immediate, highly profitable investments available to him.

Solution: True.

22-3. True or false: Reorganization is an informal equivalent to bankruptcy.

Solution: False. Assignment is an informal equivalent to bankruptcy.

22-4. Which of the following has the lowest priority of claims in the distribution of proceeds from a bankruptcy liquidation?
    a. Taxes due all governmental agencies.
    b. Cost of administering the bankrupt estate.
    c. Secured creditors.
    d. Unsecured creditors.
    e. Preferred stockholders.

Solution: e.

22-5. The financial statements of the Rathmore Paper Company for 1972 were as follows:

Rathmore Paper Company—Balance sheet, December 31, 1972
(in millions of dollars)

Current assets	$ 50	Current liabilities	$ 25
Investments	20	Advance payments for subscriptions	35
Net fixed assets	65	Reserves	5
Goodwill	15	$6 preferred stock, $60 par,	
		1,000,000 shares	60
		$8 preferred stock, no par,	
		100,000 shares, callable	
		at $100 (but fair price $50)	5
		Common stock, 1 million shares	
		at par value of $5	5
		Retained earnings	15
Total assets	$150	Total claims	$150

A recapitalization plan is proposed in which each share of the $6.00 preferred will be exchanged for one share of $1.50 preferred (stated value, $15) plus one 6 percent subordinated income debenture (stated principal, $45).

Note: The $8 preferred stock is recapitalized by drawing down the cash account of current assets (from $50 to $45 million). Notice that the trustees have decided that $50 per share is a fair price rather than the call price of $100.

a. Show the *pro forma* balance sheet giving effect to the recapitalization, showing the new preferred at its stated value and the common stock at its par value.

Solution:

Rathmore Paper Company—Pro forma balance sheet
(in millions of dollars)

Current assets	$ 45	Current liabilities	$ 25
Investments	20	Advance payments for subscriptions	35
Net fixed assets	65	Reserves	5
Goodwill	15	6% subordinated income-debentures,	
		1,000,000 at $45	45
		$1.50 preferred stock, 1,000,000	
		at $15	15
		Common stock outstanding,	
		5 million shares at $1 par	5
		Retained earnings	15
Total assets	$145		$145

b. Present the *pro forma* income statement (in millions of dollars carried to two decimal places).

Rathmore Paper Company–Consolidated statement of income and expense for year ended December 31, 1972
(in millions of dollars)

Operating income		$200.0
Operating expense		175.0
Net operating income		25.0
Other income		3.0
Other expense		0.0
Earnings before income tax		28.0
Income tax at 50%		14.0
Income after taxes		14.0
Dividends on $4.50 prior preferred stock	$6.0	
Dividends on $8.00 preferred stock	0.8	6.8
Income available for common stock		7.2

Solution:

Rathmore Paper Company
(in millions of dollars)

Net operating income		$25.00
Other income	$3.00	
Interest expense (0.06 × 45)	2.70	0.30
Earnings before income tax		25.30
Income tax, 50%		12.65
Income after taxes		12.65
Dividends on preferred stock (1.5 × 1)		1.50
Income available to common stock		$11.15

c. How much does the firm increase income available to common stock by the recapitalization?

Solution: Income available to common stock increased by (11.15 − 7.2) = 3.95 or $3,950,000.

d. How much less is the required pre-tax earnings after the recapitalization compared to those before the change? "Required earnings" is that amount which is just enough to meet fixed charges, debenture interest, and/or preferred dividends in this case.

Solution: Preferred dividends were $6.8 million. To pay these, the firm had to earn double that amount—13.6 million. After recapitalization, it need earn only the debenture expense of $2.7 million plus double the preferred dividends of $1.5 million, a total of $5.7 million, representing a reduction of 7.9 million in required earnings before interest and taxes.

Part VIII

An Integrated View of Financial Management

Chapter 23

The Timing of Financial Policy

Theme: The financial manager is not only concerned with *how* to finance, but he is also vitally concerned with *when* to finance. Since good financial timing is a result of sound judgment, it is essential that the financial manager understand the variables involved.

I. Impact of interest rates.
   A. Interest rates do not necessarily have a determining influence on investment activity. A differential impact of rates on different types of investment must be recognized:
      1. Business.
         a. Heavy industry versus light industry.
         b. Inventories versus plant and equipment.
         c. Small firms versus larger.
      2. State and local governments.
      3. Housing and construction activity.
   B. Large interest rate fluctuations, especially short-term rates, make capital costs one of the most volatile of input costs.
   C. The greatest influence of interest rates lies in their role as an index of the availability of financing. Especially for small and medium-sized firms, a period of rising interest rates may indicate increasing difficulty in obtaining financing.

II. Characteristic patterns in the cost of money.
   A. Short-term interest rates show the widest amplitude of swings and move more quickly than long-term rates.
   B. Long-term rates are not as sensitive as short-term rates. In part, long-term rates are an average of expected short-term rates over the life of the security.
   C. The cost of debt money tends generally to lag movements in general business conditions, both at the peak and the trough.
   D. The spread between long-term and short-term rates typically grows larger during a period of low growth and tends to narrow during a business upswing.

E. The cost of equity money exhibits wide fluctuations. It tends to move inversely to the cost of debt money.

III. Money and capital market behavior.

    A. Federal Reserve policy tools include:

      1. Changes in reserve requirements.

      2. Open market policy.

      3. Discount rates.

      4. Selective controls, for example, over margin requirements and consumer credit.

    B. Fiscal policy.

      1. A cash budget deficit stimulates the economy.

      2. A surplus has a restraining influence.

      3. The extent of the influence depends on how the deficit is financed or the way the surplus is used.

    C. The growth rates of GNP, the monetary stock, and government expenditures tend to move together. Inflationary expectations developed in the period since 1968.

IV. Forecasting interest rate patterns.

    A. Future movements in price levels affect interest rates in two ways.

      1. Nominal interest rates reflect expectations of future price level behavior.

      2. The outlook for inflation influences government monetary policy, which in turn affects interest rates.

    B. Demand and supply factors.

      1. The main task is to assess the future behavior of the major supply and demand factors. By projecting the sources and uses of funds in detailed individual categories, the direction of the pressure on interest rates may be estimated.

      2. For example, if the forecasted quantity demanded exceeds the indicated supply of funds (when the sum of demands and the sum of supplies are totaled at existing interest structure), interest rates are likely to go up.

    C. Sources and uses of funds.

      1. Personal savings account for over 70 percent of total savings. Contractual savings has increased to more than one-half of individual savings. Internal financing of corporate investment has declined.

      2. The principal uses of long-term funds are nonfinancial corporate bonds and stocks, real estate mortgages, and government debt. The principal uses of corporate funds have been plant and equipment, trade and consumer credit, and inventories.

      3. Forecasts of interest rates by analysis of supply and demand for funds were generally accurate until 1969.

V. Implications of fluctuations in the cost and availability of funds include the following:

    A. During a period of relatively slow growth in the economy:

      1. Short-term rates are lower than long-term rates.

2. Long-term rates, however, are low in relation to their average level.
3. Earnings-price ratios on common stocks are relatively high (P/E ratios are low).
4. Qualitative terms of debt financing will be favorable at this stage of the business cycle.
5. Therefore, long-term debt should be used to finance growth when the economy is in a slump.

B. During a period of high economic growth or strong inflationary pressures, the following can be expected:
1. Short-term rates are high—perhaps higher than long-term rates—but both long and short rates are high.
2. Availability of debt funds may be limited.
3. Terms of credit may be relatively onerous.
4. Earnings-price ratios are relatively low (if profit prospects have not deteriorated).
5. Sell equity; maybe even refund longer term debt. This reduces debt and builds equity base, facilitating the use of more debt at the beginning of the next upswing.

VI. Important changes in financing that seem to occur during a prolonged period of inflation:
A. Internal sources become less able to finance growth.
B. An increase occurs in long-term relative to short-term financing.
C. An increase occurs in public flotations of equity issues to balance to some extent the debt increases.
D. Debt ratios rise despite equity sales.
E. An increase occurs in the use of convertibles and warrants.
F. Insurance companies and other institutional lenders virtually cease to provide credit to small and medium-sized borrowers on a straight debt basis.
G. An increase occurs in the wholesaling of credit by large firms to smaller firms through trade credit.

PROBLEMS

23-1. Past experience indicated that when interest rates reach high levels smaller firms:
    a. Become quite insensitive to the interest rate.
    b. Often find funds are not available to them.
    c. Switch to commercial paper financing.
    d. Rely on their investment banking ties to fill their funds requirements.

Solution: b. The process is often called credit rationing.

23-2. Fill in the blanks with either *short-term* or *long-term* to best complete the sentences about interest rates.

a. _____ rates fluctuate less than _____ rates.
b. _____ rates reflect current supply and demand conditions for funds.
c. _____ rates reflect future expectations about the availability of funds.
d. _____ rates are (1) more volatile and (2) more sensitive to general business conditions than _____ rates.

Solution:

a. Long-term, short-term.
b. Short-term.
c. Long-term.
d. Short-term, long-term.

23-3. True or false? Firms generally wait too long into an expansionary period to raise long-term debt.

Solution: True.

23-4. After several years of excellent performance, in mid-1958 the Yaari Company made a reappraisal of its sales budgets for the next one, two, and five years. The picture looked dim for existing products, so the company initiated a product development program scheduled to run for at least the next five years. The officers decided that an annual sales growth of only 2–4 percent (on a compound basis) could be expected during the development program, but an increased rate of growth would occur thereafter.

The Yaari Company had total assets of $20 million, and its debt ratio was 60 percent at the time. Since the company planned to spend heavily on research and development during the five-year period, its profits would be depressed and the stock would be unfavorably regarded by investors. The company learned that it could borrow on a short-term basis at 2.5 percent, sell some common stock, or float nonconvertible long-term bonds at 4 percent. Yaari financed by selling $4 million of nonconvertible long-term bonds, with terms requiring a strong current ratio and limitations on fixed assets purchases.

In early 1960 investment bankers informed the company that further bond sales were not feasible because of the high level of fixed charges. However, additional financing was required for the research and development program. At this point Yaari reluctantly sold $6 million of common stock at a price of $40, down from a 1958 high of $97.

Evaluate the timing of the selections of forms of financing by the Yaari Company.

Solution: Yaari should have financed by common stock in mid-1958 because of the already high debt ratio (60 percent); the expected decline in the growth of sales and profits, which tends to limit the ability of the company to secure the heavy fixed charges; and the then-high price of the stock. Another unfavorable factor is that Yaari may find future expansion handicapped by the requirements of the debt agreement. The above situation limits the firm's use of debt financing after five years, when the development program came to fruition.

Yaari sold common stock too late. In mid-1958 the market price of the stock was near its peak, and the firm should have taken advantage of this fact.

In conclusion, it would have been better to have sold common stock before the decline in the growth rate of sales and profits, and to have built a base for later financing by long-term debt.